The Macat Library

世界思想宝库钥匙丛书

解析贾雷德·M.戴蒙德

《枪炮、病菌与钢铁：
人类社会的命运》

AN ANALYSIS OF

JARED M. DIAMOND'S

GUNS, GERMS, AND STEEL

The Fate of Human Societies

Riley Quinn ◎ 著

赵婧 ◎ 译

上海外语教育出版社
外教社 SHANGHAI FOREIGN LANGUAGE EDUCATION PRESS

MACAT

目　录

CONTENTS

引 言

要点

- 贾雷德·戴蒙德 1997 年出版的《枪炮、病菌与钢铁：人类社会的命运》，于 1998 年获得备受推崇的普利策奖＊非虚构类作品奖。
- 在《枪炮、病菌与钢铁》一书中，戴蒙德提出地理因素对历史发展有重要影响。
- 该书将时间、空间跨度巨大的历史案例放在一起进行对比，大规模使用历史分析中的比较研究法。

贾雷德·戴蒙德其人

《枪炮、病菌与钢铁：人类社会的命运》的作者贾雷德·戴蒙德 1937 年出生于波士顿，是美国进化生物学家、人类学家、生态学家和历史学家。他的父亲是儿科医生，母亲是钢琴演奏家和语言教师；戴蒙德部分受到母亲的影响，会说十二国语言。

戴蒙德先后在美国哈佛大学和英国剑桥大学攻读生物化学（研究生命体内的化学反应）和生理学（研究生理解剖结构），并由此培养了广泛的兴趣。他于 1965 年完成学业，在哈佛大学短暂工作一段时间后，出任加州大学洛杉矶分校医学院生理学教授。他的生态学研究由此开启。

他热衷于鸟类学，定期探访位于南太平洋的新几内亚岛。虽然探访的初衷是研究岛上的鸟类，但是戴蒙德渐渐对生活在那里的土著居民也产生了兴趣。与当地政治家耶利＊的偶遇，激发了他研究人类社会发展史的兴趣。在《枪炮、病菌与钢铁》一书中，戴蒙德运用以往所学，对人类社会进行分析。

65 岁时，戴蒙德彻底放弃了最初的研究领域，即医学与生理学，将全部精力倾注于环境历史与进化生物学研究。如今他是加州大学洛杉矶分校的地理学教授，同时还兼顾另两项事业：推动新几内亚环保事业发展，以及创作面向大众读者的历史书籍。

《枪炮、病菌与钢铁》的主要内容

《枪炮、病菌与钢铁》是贾雷德·戴蒙德对耶利所提出问题的探讨性回答。耶利是他探访新几内亚的旅途中遇到的一位政治家。耶利问道："为什么你们白人制造了那么多的货物（物资），并将它们运到新几内亚来，而我们黑人却几乎没有属于自己的货物呢？"[1] 耶利其实是想让戴蒙德解释"不平衡发展"*这一现象——世界范围内技术、财富、生活水平、自由程度及其他关键因素上的差异。简而言之，为什么有些国家是"发达国家"，而其他国家却是"发展中国家"？

戴蒙德对这一问题的回答聚焦于长期的历史根源。他探究和梳理了 13 000 年的历史，并据此提出当今世界的发展不平衡主要归因于 15 世纪至 19 世纪的这段历史，当时欧洲人征服了世界上大多数地区。然而戴蒙德只将欧洲国家的征服行为列为"直接"原因（即最接近的、最明显的动因）。"直接"原因并非戴蒙德探究的目标，他志在寻找造成这一问题的"根本"原因，即催生直接原因的隐性的、长期的因素。

戴蒙德发现，问题的答案与农业的出现有关。当人类放弃狩猎和采集，以农业活动为中心聚居，他们便不必跟随着季节性降雨和动物迁徙频繁迁移以解决基本的生存问题，即满足当下生存所需。迁徙性因此注定降低。最终，城镇与城市形成。狩猎—采集*社会中的每个成员，都要花费大量时间寻找食物。而在农业社会中，只需一部分人从事粮食生产；其他人可以担任领袖、书吏、士兵、铁匠、科学家等等。文字、技术等的发展需要这样的社会架构。

戴蒙德的论证并没有止步于此。他再次设问，为什么有些社会族群会先步入农业时代？为了回答**这个问题**，他从地理学入手，指出这是因为驯化*难度较小的动植物分布不均衡，绝大多数分布于欧亚大陆西南和东南地区。欧亚大陆东西轴线而非南北轴线的分布，使这一地区的植物传播及思想交流更加便利。

由于欧亚大陆拥有广袤的、自然环境相似的地区，历史上各个时期遇到的社会问题相似，因此能够借鉴和分享解决方案。而在这一区域外，能够驯化的动植物数量很少。即便狩猎—采集者族群形成了新思想，也不可能改变其生活方式。地理上的偶然因素和自然资源分布的不均衡，为现代社会贫富差异埋下了伏笔。

1997 年《枪炮、病菌与钢铁》一经出版，便掀起了世界的关注热潮，并荣获两项殊荣即普利策非虚构类作品奖和美国大学优等生荣誉学会科学图书奖（奖励在科学方面有突出贡献的书籍）。这本书被翻译成 36 种语言，成为世界各地本科生阅读清单上的必读书目。这些成就一部分归功于这本书运用了历史分析中的比较研究法：像"研究"科学一样"研究"历史。

《枪炮、病菌与钢铁》的学术价值

该书介绍了历史研究中的"比较研究法"，即运用科学论证来分析历史根源。比较研究法旨在分析为何**相近**的情况会产生**不同**的结果，而**不同**的情况会产生**相近**的结果。基于这一点，可以提出更为重要深刻的问题：两种相近的情况中包含了哪些不同因素？不同的情况中又包含了哪些相近的因素？这有助于建立**因果关系**，解释是哪个特定的因素导致了哪种特定的结果。

比较研究法是一种强有力的研究工具。几乎可以运用于所有考察因果关系的学科当中。例如，政治学研究便常用此方法来推导结论。学生可以分别分析发达与欠发达＊国家的状况，考察这些国家过去所做的政策选择，进行相互比较，以此分析国家间发展差异的原因。

比较与论证是培养批判性思维的两个关键概念。批判性思维不止步于研究那些停留在表面上的观点，而是运用一套理性体系去分析事物发展的真正原因。以非科学方法考察人类历史，是无法研究出 13 000 年前影响社会发展进程的因素的。

戴蒙德的研究不乏各种批评的声音，通过研读这些声音，也可以提升学生的批判性思维能力。虽然戴蒙德作为批判性历史学家致力于推翻他人的假设，但他也提出了自己的假设。例如，一些评论家提出，戴蒙德的作品并不如他所宣称的那样科学，他的假设存在"文化局限性"（其研究前提是西方某些关于社会"应完成什么"的理论具有普适性）。

---

1. 贾雷德·M. 戴蒙德：《枪炮、病菌与钢铁：人类社会的命运》，纽约：W. W. 诺顿出版社，1999 年，第 14 页。

第一部分：学术渊源

1 作者生平与历史背景

要点 🔑

- 《枪炮、病菌与钢铁》运用人类历史 13 000 年来的数据，对人类社会的不平等现象展开科学的研究。

- 戴蒙德在新几内亚岛的经历，促使他研究为何有些国家与其他国家相比发展滞后。

- 西方国家与苏联之间冷战 * 的结束和全球化 * 的兴起（世界各国经济、人口和文化联系紧密）引起了人们对这类问题的热烈讨论。

为何要读这部著作？

贾雷德·戴蒙德的《枪炮、病菌与钢铁》一书研究了多种历史演进模式背后的根本原因。他提出，在人类过去 13 000 年的历史中，不同民族发展道路迥异的原因在于各大陆板块自然环境的差异，而非人种间的生物学差异。欧洲人为何能征服美洲，本书标题揭示了这一问题的直接原因。但是戴蒙德坚信，我们不能只满足于这些答案，而是应当顺着因果关系，找到导致这些直接原因发生的根本原因，即大陆板块间的环境差异以及粮食产量的增加。

他试图运用一种科学的研究方法来探讨人类历史，从不同学科中汲取观点并进行整合，推导出了有关人类发展的广义理论。他借用生物学研究中的比较研究法，考证自己那些"跨越时空、无须环境处理的社会发展模式"。[1] 换句话说，他将时空跨度巨大的历史环境相互对比，以此发现不同结果背后的缘由。

他的研究并非只停留于揭示影响权力与财富积累的显性因素，

即枪炮、病菌与钢铁，而是探究更深层次的"因果关系"来寻找答案。根据他的理论，人类社会发展不平衡的根本原因在于各个大陆板块之间的环境差异以及利于或不利于粮食产量与生产面积增加的条件。

通过《枪炮、病菌与钢铁》一书可见，在研究人类历史那些至关重要的问题时，采用涉及面广、大胆的跨学科研究方法是可行的。

> "贫富差距究竟有多大，现状如何？简单回答如下：世界上最富有的工业化国家如瑞士，与最贫穷的非工业化国家如莫桑比克相比，人均收入之比为 400 : 1。"
>
> —— 戴维·兰德斯：《国富国穷》

作者生平

1937 年，贾雷德·戴蒙德出生于波士顿。母亲是一位音乐家和语言学爱好者，父亲是哈佛大学医学院附属波士顿儿童医院的副院长和血液疾病专家。戴蒙德曾在哈佛大学主修生物化学。读书期间，他的理想一直是成为父亲那样的内科医生。本科学习最后一年，他的研究兴趣转向生物学研究，后在英国剑桥大学获得生理学博士学位。

第二次世界大战*对戴蒙德世界观的形成有重要影响。博士毕业后，他游历欧洲，观察人们的战争经历如何影响了他们的生活。戴蒙德指出，"依据他们是英国人、德国人、芬兰人或是南斯拉夫人，出生于 1937 年的我，可以马上判断出他们的生活是否经受过重大的挫折"，如父母亡故、家园被毁等。他认为，"一个人出生于伦敦、柏林、赫尔辛基或是萨格勒布，完全是偶然的"。[2] 戴蒙德的思考关注了环境对个人机遇的影响，这对其日后的研究有重要的启发。

1964 年，他前往太平洋新几内亚岛旅行。在那里，他的研究重心从医学实验转向生态学和生物学。戴蒙德对新几内亚岛上的野生动植物和土著居民越来越感兴趣，研究生涯也由此改变。他早期对医学和解剖学的关注，逐渐扩展至历史学、地理学、生态学、生物学以及人类学。虽然从未接受过这些领域的专业训练，但是自70 年代起戴蒙德先后 26 次前往新几内亚做实地调查，并陆续发表了多篇相关论文。

创作背景

20 世纪 90 年代中期，戴蒙德创作了《枪炮、病菌与钢铁》一书。从 1945 年到 1989 年，在他一生的多数时光里，世界政治格局都沉浸在美国与苏联的冷战与对抗关系中。

冷战后的一段时间，发达国家与发展中国家之间以及发展中国家之间新的政治关系变得更为重要。"我们生活在动荡的时代。"1990 年联合国 *《人类发展报告》如是开篇。"在那些民主长期受到压制的国家里"，政治体系与经济结构"开始转变"[3]。换句话说，发达国家与发展中国家的联系将逐步增多，重要性也日益突出，于是便产生了比如为何有些国家依旧贫困、为此我们该做些什么这样的问题。

几乎在《枪炮、病菌与钢铁》出版的同时，美国经济学家、历史学家戴维·兰德斯 * 的《国富国穷》一书也面市了，解释了寻找社会发展不均衡原因这项课题的迫切性与重要性。他提出，"以往将世界划分为东方与西方两大阵营的想法，已过时了"，意识形态对峙与潜在的核战危险后，"人类所面临的巨大挑战与威胁是贫富群体之间财富与健康的差距"。[4] 若要解决人类社会发展进程中的诸多问题以及不均衡发展的现象，应首先找出这些问题与现象的根本成因。戴蒙德与兰德斯都力图挖掘其中的根本原因。

---

1. 克里斯托弗·米勒："评贾雷德·M.戴蒙德的《枪炮、病菌与钢铁：人类社会的命运》"，《经济植物学》第 56 卷，2002 年第 2 期，第 209 页。

2. 贾雷德·戴蒙德："自我介绍"，登录日期 2015 年 5 月 30 日，http://www.jareddiamond.org/Jared_Diamond/About_Me.html。

3. 马赫布卜·哈克编：《1990 年人类发展报告》，纽约：牛津大学出版社，1990 年，第 iii 页。

4. 戴维·兰德斯：《国富国穷：为什么有的国家如此富有而有的国家如此贫穷》，纽约：W. W. 诺顿出版社，1998 年，第 xx 页。

2 学术背景

要点 🔑

- "人地关系"＊地理学主要研究人类与环境之间的关系。

- 英国著名博物学家查尔斯·达尔文＊（1859 年发表了进化论）和法国历史学家费尔南·布罗代尔＊（历史年鉴学派＊创始人）在他们的著作中，运用了自然科学研究方法，来分析潜在因素与结果之间的关系。

- 自然科学的研究方法可应用到其他相关的社会科学学科中，如过程主义考古学＊（旨在确立人类行为的"定律"，从而对考古文物作出阐释）及环境社会学（旨在理解自然环境中人类的社会行为）。

著作语境

贾雷德·戴蒙德的《枪炮、病菌与钢铁》是一本跨学科著作，它汲取了不同学科的研究目标及方法。虽然，这本书与历史学、政治学及物理学相关，但与之联系更为紧密的是地理学。

美国地理学家威廉·D. 帕蒂森＊提出，地理学研究有四大传统：空间传统、区域研究传统、地球科学传统和人地关系传统。"空间"传统将不同事物的"距离、形态、方向、位置"进行比较，主要关注地图以及陆地形态。"区域研究"传统着重于考察物理形态之外"区域的本质、特征和区别"，通常致力于描述社会政治差异，而非分析其根源。"地球科学"传统如地理学研究，运用物理学和化学来分析物质世界。[2] 而在这四大传统中，戴蒙德的书属于"人地关系"传统。

"人地关系地理学"研究通常包括社会学研究（考察人类社会历史及发展运作的学科），探讨地（地理学）与人（社会学）的相互影响，进而分析这些影响如何塑造各个时期的历史事件（历史学）。结构主义*是研究人类文化的一种方法，其思想基础在于人类的行为受其所处的地域影响，并囊括于一个更大的系统中[3]。结构主义对人地关系研究至关重要。而在戴蒙德看来，这一更大系统中的重要因素是环境。

> "新（过程主义）考古学强调在寻找人类行为的一般规律时，应重视理论形成、模型建构及假设检验。过程主义考古学最为重要的贡献在于它对文化过程而非文化历史的重视。"
>
> —— 蒂莫西·K. 厄尔和罗伯特·W. 普瑞塞尔：
> "过程主义考古学与激进批判"

学科概览

英国博物学家查尔斯·达尔文在其具有深远影响力的《物种起源》（1859）一书中，阐释了动植物与自然环境之间的关系。书中提出的自然选择*学说讲述了自然环境如何通过"优胜劣汰"[4]影响生物特征。这一观点对于自然环境所扮演的角色的理解，与我们正在讨论的话题息息相关。达尔文认为，经历时间的淘洗，自然环境会决定谁是"优胜者"，谁是"淘汰者"。这一观点被用来（有时是误用）解释人类社会各种各样的变化与发展。

美国地理学家埃尔斯沃思·亨廷顿*的著作《文明与气候》（1915）便误用了达尔文的观点。亨廷顿在书中指出，气候与人类社会有一定联系，"极北地区和沙漠地区人口稀少、发展落后的原因很简单，人们长期为艰难的生存环境所桎梏，隔绝于世"。[5] 亨廷顿意在将特定的文化与人们在所处地域的生存需求相联系。然而在他强调种族的作用，将"条顿人"（德语母语者）与"黑人"（带有非洲血统的人）相比较时，论证便出了问题。他认为"就如李子跟苹果，两者不仅外观、形状和颜色不同，内里的味道也不同，因此黑人和白人……的思维方式也不同"。[6] 认为深肤色的种族天生比白人低下、他们的文明也注定落后的观点，盛行了数个世纪，为欧洲帝国侵略扩张开脱。

人们常将法国历史学家费尔南·布罗代尔与年鉴学派联系在一起，年鉴学派的名称源于布罗代尔参与编辑的一本历史研究杂志。相比之下，布罗代尔与年鉴学派的视野相对来说更加开阔。他们分析了长时段*历史这一概念——导致历史事件发生的长期而隐秘的因素，以及那些演变缓慢，缓慢到几乎无法察觉的因素（比如说，森林的渐渐消逝将影响当地经济发展，反过来又将助推新政权的上位）。

在布罗代尔看来，"人类生活的大环境"并非国王的法令，而是半岛、海洋和高山，即塑造人类行为的是非人为的因素。布罗代尔具有开创价值的著作《菲利普二世时代的地中海世界》（1949），在开篇分析了 16 世纪地中海地区的**自然**环境。虽然布罗代尔在这本书中重点研究的历史时期很短，只是从 1550 年至 1600 年，但是他的研究对象都来源于"多个不同时期、区域的考古证据、影像和地貌"。[7]

学术渊源

自然环境决定社会结构，从而影响社会发展，戴蒙德深受这一观念的影响。在他的书中，戴蒙德将这一观念应用到考古学当中。美国人类学家朱利安·斯图尔德 * 是一位过程主义考古学派学者，认为考古研究应更多地借助科学而非历史研究方法。他写道："每个人都要吃饭，这是生物本能，而不是一项文化事实……不同群族的人所吃的食物和进食方式不同，这是文化事实，而且只能从文化史和自然环境因素的角度来解释。"[8]

过程主义考古学不仅关注那些"生物本能"，还关注"文化事实"。举例来说，生物本能可以指人类食用小麦这一事实；而文化事实则指的是食用小麦对人类来说**意味**着什么以及我们能够从中了解到古代农业的哪些特征。过程主义考古学并不是将考古学视为一扇瞥见静态历史的窗户，而是将它视为一系列线索，能够从中推断出古代人的生活状态，总结人类行为的总体特征。

除了过程主义考古学，戴蒙德还受到了环境社会学的影响。环境社会学科的推动者美国社会学家赖利·邓拉普 * 和威廉·卡顿 * 认为，环境社会学研究"包含的理念是，自然环境影响人类社会和人类行为，反之亦然"。[9]社会学研究出现了新的转变，而在此之前，社会学一直注重考察人类不同族群间的联系。将环境因素纳入研究范畴并将其视为一项全新的变量，促使"人地关系"地理学研究与社会学研究交叉融合。

---

1. 威廉·D. 帕蒂森："地理学研究的四大传统"，《地理学杂志》第 63 卷，1964 年第 5 期，第 211—216 页。

2. 帕蒂森："地理学研究的四大传统"，第 211—216 页。

3. 帕蒂森："地理学研究的四大传统"。

4. 查尔斯·达尔文：《物种起源》，牛津：牛津大学出版社，2008 年，第 64 页。

5. 埃尔斯沃思·亨廷顿：《文明与气候》，康涅狄格州纽黑文：耶鲁大学出版社，1915 年，第 2 页。

6. 亨廷顿：《文明与气候》，第 16 页。

7. 费尔南·布罗代尔：《菲利普二世时代的地中海世界（第一卷）》，伦敦：加利福尼亚大学出版社，1995 年，第 23 页。

8. 朱利安·斯图尔德：《文化变迁理论：多线进化方法论》，芝加哥：伊利诺伊大学出版社，1972 年，第 8 页。

9. 赖利·邓拉普和威廉·卡顿："环境社会学"，《社会学年鉴》第 5 卷，1979 年，第 244 页。

3 主导命题

要点 🔑

- 既然地球上每个种族的人都是一样的（没有哪个族群的人具有天然的智力和创造力优势），那么为何不同国家发展状况不平衡就成了学术界常常讨论的问题。

- 世界体系理论*将地区发展欠发达归因于其他民族的压迫；其他许多有关不均衡发展的理论则认为原因在于17世纪时欧洲与其他地区的发展差距。

- 戴蒙德考察了更为久远的历史。他认为，将原因归咎于17世纪时的社会状况是错误的，应当在史前时期寻找答案。

核心问题

如我们所知，贾雷德·戴蒙德将一位新几内亚人耶利的提问作为《枪炮，病菌与钢铁》的核心问题。耶利是戴蒙德的朋友，是当地的政治家。耶利问道："为什么你们白人制造了那么多的货物（物资），并将它们运到新几内亚来，而我们黑人却几乎没有属于自己的货物呢？"[1]耶利问的是，为何世界上一部分地区经济发展迅速，而另一些地区则与之相反。20世纪后半叶，随着全球化进程的不断推进，即世界各地在文化、经济和政治上互相交融，这一问题也变得越来越重要。

尽管经济发展水平各异，但不同文化间的交流却越来越密切和频繁，因此找到发展不均衡的原因至关重要。身为科学家的戴蒙德，不满足于将这一问题简单化，或从技术、智力、文化等方面寻找多少有些冒犯性的答案。他选择了更为严谨的研究方法。因此，戴蒙德的问题并不是"为什么会出现贫富不均？"，而是"导致贫富不均的那些因素的源头在哪里？"正是这一问题让戴蒙德将研究范围回溯至 13 000 年前。

> "东方文明的浩瀚冲击了欧洲的想象，其恢宏壮观显而易见，有庄严雄伟的土木工程建筑，还有气派豪华的宫苑。但机械工程却迟滞不前，普通民众生活穷困……总而言之，这些国家平均收入不高，在这一指标上远低于欧洲。"
>
> —— 埃里克·琼斯：《欧洲奇迹》

参与者

一些关注这个问题的学者倾向于认为，欧洲确立主导地位与其他国家的发展拉开差距主要出现在 16、17 世纪这段时间。

伊曼纽尔·沃勒斯坦 * 的"世界体系理论"是解释发展不均衡的重要理论之一。该理论根据一国是否为另一国的繁荣发展提供劳动力来区分"核心"与"边缘"国家。"15 世纪末 16 世纪初，"沃勒斯坦提出，"一个我们所说的欧洲世界经济体正逐步崭露头角。"[2] 由此，欧洲核心国家和非欧洲的边缘国家间开始出现劳动分工。他指出："在渐渐成型的世界经济体系中，地缘经济上处于边缘的地区有两项主要的社会活动：采矿与务农。"这些地区的矿产资源和农产品最终将回到核心地区。[3]

沃勒斯坦在西欧资本主义 * 意识形态中找到了这一问题的根源。按照资本主义理论，从事劳动的人常常使用获利者所拥有的资源和工具开展工作。因此资本主义的产生需要两方的存在：资产阶级和工人阶级。

英裔澳大利亚经济历史学家埃里克·琼斯*在其重要著作《欧洲奇迹》（1981）中指出（与费尔南·布罗代尔和沃勒斯坦的观点一致），16 世纪是决定欧洲占据世界主导地位的时期，那时欧洲大陆"正值政治、技术和地理探索的快速发展期，也由此成为工业世界的诞生地"。[4] 从地理环境到政治架构，欧洲快速发展的因素是多方位的。

16 世纪以来，欧洲大陆技术的快速发展是独特的现象，琼斯认为："这一体系中各国间的文化联系与相互竞争，促使彼此之间不断借鉴经验教训与'刺激扩散'，也即面对同一问题，只要一个国家找到了解决方法，其他国家便可效仿，问题迎刃而解。"[5] 换句话说，欧洲大陆的国家足够独立，可以相互竞争，但同时联系也足够紧密，使得在面对同样问题时，可学习其他国家的经验。这种对人与地关系的分析，是琼斯惯用的研究方法。

当代论战

戴蒙德在《枪炮、病菌与钢铁》中写到，他的论点与那些建立在种族主义伪科学——用科学话语阐释不科学的观点——上的观点截然不同，如埃尔斯沃思·亨廷顿*的观点。"也许最常见的阐释"欧洲与其他地区发展不均衡的观点，他写道，"不管含蓄的、直率的，其论证都建立在种族间存在生理上的差异这一预设上"。[6] 戴蒙德其实不是针对那些内含隐晦种族歧视观念的学术论点；几十年前这些论点已被唾弃。他抨击的是学界外也广泛存在的文化偏见。

20 世纪下半叶，戴蒙德的书的知名度远超同时期其他书籍。与多数学术著作不同，《枪炮、病菌与钢铁》语言通俗易懂，没有引用任何文献。事实上，对这本书的其中一项批评便是，它几乎没有参与到当时的地理学、历史学、考古学讨论中去。[7]

那么戴蒙德到底是在向谁发起挑战？他质疑的是那些将不均衡发展追溯到15、16世纪"某一时期"欧洲在人口、食物产量和技术方面远远领先其他地区因而出现分流的论点。然而这仅仅是问题的部分答案。戴蒙德坚信，社会发展差异的根源以及根源背后的潜在原因，还没有人进行过透彻研究。

1. 贾雷德·M.戴蒙德：《枪炮、病菌与钢铁：人类社会的命运》，纽约：W.W.诺顿出版社，1999年，第14页。
2. 伊曼纽尔·沃勒斯坦：《现代世界体系（第一卷）：16世纪资本主义农业及欧洲世界经济的起源》，伦敦：加利福尼亚大学出版社，2011年，第15页。
3. 沃勒斯坦：《现代世界体系》，第100页。
4. 埃里克·琼斯：《欧洲奇迹：欧亚史中的环境、经济和地缘政治》，剑桥：剑桥大学出版社，2003年，第225页。
5. 琼斯：《欧洲奇迹》，第45页。
6. 戴蒙德：《枪炮、病菌与钢铁》，第18—19页。
7. 理查德·约克和菲利普·曼库斯："璞玉之思：论戴蒙德《枪炮、病菌与钢铁》"，《人类生态学研究》第14卷，2007年第2期，第159页。

4 作者贡献

要点 &

- 戴蒙德认为，现代社会发展不均衡的根源在于地理因素，在农业文明尚未出现的 13 000 年前，地理环境是唯一会导致社会分化的因素。

- 戴蒙德的研究通过进行多项自然实验 *——将生活在不同环境中的人群进行比较，以探究不同族群命运迥异的原因——结合了多个不同的学科如地理学、考古学、社会学等等的知识。

- 人类发展问题一直是 20 世纪的研究热点，戴蒙德拓宽了这一问题的规模与范围。

作者目标

在《枪炮、病菌与钢铁》一书中，戴蒙德用一句话总结了他的核心观点："不同的人类族群有着不同的历史发展轨迹，原因在于他们所处自然环境不同，而非族群之间的生物学差异。"[1]

然而戴蒙德这本书主要的关注点，不只是推翻人种间"生物学"差异理论，更是意在超越那些"只解开了部分谜团，却……欠缺全面考量的观点"[2]，展开更加深入的研究。这是对历史的"结构主义"*探索，关注非人为的因素怎样影响和塑造了人的行为。

西方为何能够占据优势地位？戴蒙德意在找到这一问题的根本原因，而非直接原因。为了达成这一目的，戴蒙德不得不追溯促成西方占据支配地位的各种根本性因素。他认为，如果仅将西方的主导地位归结于技术水平的领先，那么这项分析可以说是不彻底的。

如果是技术领先促使西方占据主导地位，那么又是什么因素让西方得以实现技术领先呢？若不考察 13 000 年前的历史、追溯人类文明产生的开端，这一问题便无法回答。而人类文明的开端远早于 15 世纪，15 世纪只是远古时期埋下的根源所带来的结果开始在殖民地显现出影响的时期。

> "在历史学科中，自然实验或比较研究是十分有效的研究手段。这一方法将不同的系统进行比较，这些系统具有许多相似的特征，但在研究者想要探究其影响的变量因素上却存在不同。"
>
> —— 贾雷德·戴蒙德和詹姆斯·罗宾逊：《历史的自然试验》

研究方法

在《枪炮、病菌与钢铁》一书中，贾雷德·戴蒙德运用科学的研究方法来探究历史，通过切实的考古和自然环境物证来佐证其观点。戴蒙德在书的开篇阐述了"从人类作为物种出现到 13 000 年前数百万年来各大陆地板块上人类历史的发展"[3]，旨在"将人类历史视作一门科学，使其与天文学、地质学和进化生物学等公认的历史科学学科处于同等地位"[4]。

戴蒙德无法在实验室中对不同族群进行可控的实验，因此他充分利用了"自然实验"方法，比较在某一方面存在不同的两个族群，如一个农业社会族群与另一个没有发展农业的族群。[5] 于是，戴蒙德的一些对比研究被推向了更为广阔的层面，以大陆板块为单位，考察植被、动物种群、气候或其他因素不同的区域。他利用这些因素得出结论，解释为何一些社会能拥有集中制的、复杂的社会结构和先进技术，而其他社会却做不到这一点。他考察了自然遗迹，如植物和动物的残骸化石以辨认人们在什么时候、什么地方培植了哪些农作物。

他常常利用自然物证（具有易驯化且生长速度快的特征），推导出社会科学方面的结论（能够驯养家畜的文明，通常更有发展优势），且以比较研究方法作为论证的基础。

时代贡献

戴蒙德并不是第一位探究不同人类社会为何发展状况各异的人地关系地理学家（通过分析历史事件发生的地理环境来佐证研究），也并非第一位从遥远的史前时期挖掘其根本原因的学者。

美国历史学家艾尔弗雷德·克罗斯比 * 在其 1972 年出版的著作《哥伦布大交换》中回顾了旧世界（亚洲、非洲、欧洲）和新世界（美洲、澳洲）之间跨越大陆板块的交换过程。克罗斯比对新旧世界相遇的阐释与戴蒙德的观点有许多相似之处。"当哥伦布 * 抵达时，即便是美洲大陆最为发达的土著部落，也还未走出石器时代 *，西班牙征服者 * 只派了一小队人便横扫土著的军队。"* 此外，当地的土著部落"几乎没有驯养家畜"，一些在旧世界寻常的疾病，在这里"致死率却非常高"。[6]

然而，克罗斯比对欧洲人占据世界主导地位原因的探索，只是他研究重心的一小部分。这本书的核心在于追踪千年来分离独立互不干扰的两块大陆突然间发生沟通往来后产生了怎样的影响；其中许多体现在生物学上：一些物种灭绝，另一些则扩散至全球。也就是说，克罗斯比更热衷于研究强大的欧洲人是如何跨越大洋将他们培育的植物和动物带到美洲，又是如何把美洲的珍奇品种带回自己的国家。

而戴蒙德关注更多的则是促使欧洲人占据支配地位的一系列原始条件。因此，虽然戴蒙德的书与克罗斯比的有诸多相似之处，但其贡献在于理论阐释中所展现的宏大规模与范畴。

---

1. 贾雷德·M.戴蒙德：《枪炮、病菌与钢铁：人类社会的命运》，纽约：W. W.诺顿出版社，1999 年，第 25 页。
2. 戴蒙德：《枪炮、病菌与钢铁》，第 24 页。
3. 戴蒙德：《枪炮、病菌与钢铁》，第 37 页。
4. 戴蒙德：《枪炮、病菌与钢铁》，第 408 页。
5. 戴蒙德：《枪炮、病菌与钢铁》，第 424 页。
6. 艾尔弗雷德·W.克罗斯比：《哥伦布大交换：1492 年以后的生物影响和文化冲击》，康涅狄格州韦斯特波特：普雷格出版社，2003 年，第 21 页。

第二部分：学术思想

5 思想主脉

要点 ⚿

- 《枪炮、病菌与钢铁》一书的核心主题除了全球范围内自然物资的分布以及各区域的地理特征外，还有这些资源在促进农业发展中所起到的作用，以及农业在推动社会发展中所产生的影响。

- 欧亚大陆拥有丰富多样的农作物、家畜和适宜的地理环境，促使人们在城市定居，也由此发展出了复杂的产品（枪炮与钢铁）和强大的免疫系统（病菌），而世界其他地方则不具备这些条件。

- 戴蒙德这本书的读者对象定位为普通大众，而非专家学者，也因此遭到一些批评，被指责书本内容不够严谨。

核心主题

贾雷德·戴蒙德《枪炮、病菌与钢铁》一书的重要主题关乎人类文明中最为基本的一些构成要素。其中最为核心的是农作物如容易培植的小麦等作物和驯养难度较低的山羊等家畜自然分布不均衡。农业资源分布的不均衡，意味着生活在不同地区的族群经历了不同的发展路径。

戴蒙德研究的总体问题是：世界不同地区发展不均衡的根本原因是什么？他探索的主题均与自然相关——农作物、动物和地理环境。在欧亚大陆，这些因素促使社会走向多样化发展，也催生了一些疾病的出现和扩散，也由此奠定了这些社会特别是西欧地区占据世界主导地位的基础。

了解了戴蒙德创作《枪炮、病菌与钢铁》一书的目的，便意味着也理解了"直接"原因和"根本"原因的区别。比如一颗苹果从树上落下，直接原因是一阵疾风吹过，而根本原因则需解释为何只有这只苹果落下而附近树上的其他苹果却没有落下；也许是掉苹果的这棵树生长在贫瘠的土地上，营养不良，果实根茎不如其他树结实。直接原因和根本原因都有道理，但根本原因分析得更为综合全面。

> "当皮泽洛*和阿塔瓦尔帕*在卡哈马卡*交锋时，为何是皮泽洛俘虏了阿塔瓦尔帕并杀死了他的诸多随从，而不是拥有众多军队的阿塔瓦尔帕俘虏并处死皮泽洛？毕竟，皮泽洛只有 62 位骑兵和 106 位步兵，而阿塔瓦尔帕却拥有八万兵力。"
>
> —— 贾雷德·戴蒙德：《枪炮、病菌与钢铁》

思想探究

戴蒙德总的论点是，当今世界发展不均衡的根本原因在于自然地理上的差异，而非人种间的基因差异，如某些种族的人智力天生高于其他种族。地理环境的差异包括适于被人类培植和驯化的农作物和动物（为满足人类需求进行选种培育、驯化野生动植物的过程）的差异，以及不同区域间地理特征的差异。

例如，欧洲人之所以长于战事，是因为欧洲大陆被山脉、河流天然地分隔成一块块狭小的区域，彼此间容易发生冲突。欧洲人不必打猎，也不必在大自然中觅食，肥沃的土地和丰富的淡水资源令"食物生产"更加容易，这些要素是"发展枪炮、病菌与钢铁的间接先决条件"[1]。

戴蒙德提出，食物生产并不是由世界上那些擅于打猎、采集食物的聪明人"发明"的，而是自然界缓慢"演化"的产物。[2]其源头有几大因素。其一就是获取易培育植物的便利性。如燕麦几乎不需要选择育种，人工种植十分容易，而玉米相对来说就麻烦多了。经人工培植，农作物产量可以大大提升。再如，狗经驯化后，成为对主人温顺友好的动物。

欧亚大陆天然拥有多种栽培难度较低的农作物如小麦、大麦、扁豆等，而美洲大陆则没有这样的条件。此外，完备的配套条件也使狩猎采集向农业生产的转变具有较高的价值，如足够高产的禾谷类作物、适于在田地里劳作的大型家畜（最终也有可能成为食物来源）以及温带气候*条件。戴蒙德指出，"印第安人之所以不培植苹果，原因在于他们可以轻易获取丰富的野生动植物食材"；因此他们驯养动植物的动力便减少了很多。[3]培植和驯化动植物会引起生活方式的根本性改变，因此这项活动必须有足够的价值和意义，人们才会这样去做。

食物生产是怎样促使枪炮、病菌与钢铁出现的呢？食物生产可以提高人口密度，反过来也"直接导致了病菌、文字、技术与集权政体的产生"，令欧亚大陆的民族占据世界霸主地位。[4]当人类与动物之间近距离接触、城市居民密集地生活在一起时，疾病能够轻松地跨物种传播，并迅速扩散蔓延到整个片区的人群中（比如天花最先是由牛流行传播起来的）。[5]不过，人口密度的增大，除了利于病菌扩散，还有利于技术的提升。农业社会里"充足的食物储备可以供养得起……全职的专业从业人员"，如国王、官员、铁匠、学者和士兵等。[6]相反，在狩猎采集社会中，人人都必须在寻找和加工食物上花费大量时间。因此，农业社会的抄写员和铁匠有足够的时间开展新发明如书写体系、工具和武器，从而为更为先进的发明奠定基础。

戴蒙德把这一现象称为"自我催化",指事物依靠自身发展的过程。青铜工具让人类有了更先进的工具来开采铁矿,制造更加先进的工具。由此我们便能够了解食物生产如何"促使复杂多样的社会产生的可能性"[7]。欧亚大陆天然拥有优渥的地理环境,利于食物生产。这一因素促进了技术水平的提升,而这又催生更加先进的技术,以及与其他复杂社会的思想交流——这些又将促进社会更进一步的发展。

语言表述

《枪炮、病菌与钢铁》一书的读者对象为普通大众,书评大多称赞其"博学多识,文风清晰明快,从考古学到动物学,旁征博引"[8]。戴蒙德运用了众多丰富生动的例证来透彻地解释学术观点,语句简洁明晰。他还在书中绘制了多张图表来阐释复杂的概念。尤其珍贵的是,他将所阐述的历史发展的种种根本原因进行汇总,将全书观点浓缩为一页篇幅的图表[9]。

虽然该书可读性和趣味性较强,但是也有评论者提出批评,认为这本书缺少学术文献的引用。尽管戴蒙德在书末列出了一个"延伸阅读书目表",但是正文中却几乎没有什么引证。一些评论家认为《枪炮、病菌与钢铁》收集的事实资料有误,作者的注意力全放在了言辞表述上,以吸引大众读者(还有文学奖项的评委),问题论证却有欠严谨[10]。

《枪炮、病菌与钢铁》的读者需牢记,戴蒙德一直尝试在市场吸引力和学术严谨性之间找到平衡。

1. 贾雷德·M.戴蒙德:《枪炮、病菌与钢铁：人类社会的命运》，纽约：W. W.诺顿出版社，1999 年，第 86 页。

2. 戴蒙德:《枪炮、病菌与钢铁》，第 104 页。

3. 戴蒙德:《枪炮、病菌与钢铁》，第 156 页。

4. 戴蒙德:《枪炮、病菌与钢铁》，第 195 页。

5. 戴蒙德:《枪炮、病菌与钢铁》，第 207 页。

6. 戴蒙德:《枪炮、病菌与钢铁》，第 90 页。

7. 戴蒙德:《枪炮、病菌与钢铁》，第 286 页。

8. 罗宾·麦凯:"贾雷德·戴蒙德：我们能从部落生活中学到什么"，《卫报》，2013 年 1 月 6 日，登录日期 2015 年 7 月 15 日，http://www.theguardian.com/science/2013/jan/06/jared-diamond-tribal-life-anthropology。

9. 戴蒙德:《枪炮、病菌与钢铁》，第 87 页。

10. 安德鲁·斯拉特:"新环境决定论、思想文化损害控制和自然 / 社会科学"，《对映体》第 35 卷，2003 年第 4 期，第 813 页。

6 思想支脉

要点 &⊶

- 欧亚大陆能在世界上占据主导地位，是因为其丰富的自然资源；欧洲能在欧亚大陆占据主导地位，是因为其自身的地理特征。

- 中国地理结构的一体性和政治统一，使得社会发展存在不确定性；帝王错误的决定几乎没有被修正或逆转的可能。

- 虽然人们记住更多的是《枪炮、病菌与钢铁》一书的内容而非其研究方法，但是近来越来越多的学者开始关注自然实验。

其他思想

《枪炮、病菌与钢铁》的核心主题是探究基于自然环境因素的全球历史发展。戴蒙德还研究了旧世界各区域的发展为何存在差异，尤其是中国和非洲。毕竟，旧世界在地理上相互关联，非洲和中国都出现了农业文明。

然而，还有一个关键因素，那就是东西轴向的优势。"若沿南北轴线行走，"戴蒙德写道，"所经过的区域地理差异极大，"这主要体现在气候、动植物种类和地形特征方面。这一原因阻碍了驯化的动植物和技术在南北方之间的传播。而沿东西轴线行走，各地区的气候大致稳定统一，交流也更加顺畅便捷。[1]

这一发现引导戴蒙德转向了另一有趣的问题。欧洲和中国都坐落在欧亚大陆的东西轴线上，都有丰富的食物供给和迅速的技术进步。为何只有欧洲占据了统治地位？要回答这一问题，戴蒙德将研究视角转向探索复杂社会中地理是如何影响政治的。

> "更大的面积或更多的人口意味更多的潜在发明者，更多的相互竞争的社会，更多的可以采用的发明创造，以及更大的采用和保有发明创造的压力，因为任何社会如果不这样做就往往会被竞争对手所淘汰。"
>
> —— 贾雷德·戴蒙德：《枪炮、病菌与钢铁》

思想探究

"直到公元 1450 年左右，"戴蒙德指出，"在技术发展方面，中国比欧洲更富于革新精神，也更为先进，然而自此之后，中国的技术革新就开始走下坡路。"[2] 戴蒙德列出了多条利于欧洲社会技术发展的直接原因：商人阶层与资本主义经济体系的发展；对发明创造的专利保护；相对较少出现建立在绝对专制 *（即权力集中在极少数人手里）和严苛税制基础上的政体；希腊-犹太-基督教传统的经验主义 *探究精神[3]（即把结论建立于对事物的观察之上的科学研究传统）。

同样，戴蒙德指出，隐藏在这些直接原因背后的根本原因是地理因素，而政治上的统一也是其关键所在。中国是一个大一统的国家。这意味着一时的"倒退"或错误的决定会造成永久的伤害。戴蒙德举了一个例子，15 世纪时中国朝廷因一场政治纷争而永久废除了海洋舰队。[4] 而欧洲在政治上相对分散，因此如果一个政体做了错误的决定，其他政体会从中吸取教训。此处，戴蒙德以意大利探险家克里斯托弗·哥伦布为例进行了说明，欧洲大陆有几百位王子，哥伦布在失败了四次后，终于说服第五位王子出资支持他去大西洋航行探险。[5]

也就是说，中国的政治体制决定了统治阶层所犯的错误会覆盖到整个国家，而欧洲的政治结构则意味着虽然前几位王子不看好哥伦布的冒险，但总会碰到一个支持者。之后，当其他人意识到首航的成功时，他们将自然而然地选择"最佳惯例"，紧随成功者的脚步。

是什么样的地理因素导致欧洲政局相对分散？欧洲大陆被众多河流、半岛、岛屿和山脉等天然屏障分隔，因此"欧洲有许多分散的面积较小的核心地区，没有一个大到足以长期控制其他地区，而每一个地区都是历史上一些独立国家的中心"。[6]而中国的岛屿数量没有那么多，且面积相对较小，在公元前221年便实现国家大一统。欧洲大陆各区域间相互分隔的地理条件，使其直到20世纪才开启统一化的进程，甚至直到现在这一进程也前途未卜。[7]戴蒙德认为，早期中国的统一是优势，可以集中大量资源去建设复杂、先进的社会。而欧洲的结构意味着"如果一个国家不进行某项革新，而另一个国家进行了革新，那么临近的国家也就不得不效仿"，否则就要面临经济、军事上的控制。

被忽视之处

在论证与结构方面，《枪炮、病菌与钢铁》篇章衔接紧凑。有鉴于此，比起内容，这本书所采用的"以科学思维对待历史"的方法论，在某种程度上被忽视了。

美国心理学家斯图尔特·维斯*提出，戴蒙德以科学视角阐释不同社会的发展结果，值得其他学科借鉴。他说，行为分析"可以引入公共对话研究领域，假如更多的行为分析师能够以戴蒙德的方法为指导进行科学的病例分析的话"。[9]维斯指出，"诸如攻击、犯罪、酗酒和吸毒等"源于行为而非基因的社会问题，可能是受到了某些"亟待发现"的重要环境因素的影响。[10]在维斯看来，戴蒙德使用的宏观比较方法，是一种无须实验室环境*就可以探求社会现实真相的方法。虽然社会学分析中"自然实验"的传统由来已久，如今也充分运用到了政策分析当中，但维斯指出，是戴蒙德证明了它可以在更为广阔的领域中得到运用，他在此方面贡献颇多。

其中一个例子是戴维·汉弗莱*和牛津大学其他同事一同进行的一项自然实验。他们使用已有数据，评估英国曼彻斯特颁布的一项售酒令的效果，研究这条管控酒水销售时段法令的废除是否会导致反社会行为的多发。法令颁布前后警方的案件报告，提供了衡量这一变化的途径。他们最终得出的结论是，法令废除后，后半夜发生的案件数量有所提高（但案件总数却没有增长）。这并非一项可控实验，而是一项"自然"实验，它利用了更为广阔的现实世界，来探寻社会现象的直接和根本原因。[11]

1. 贾雷德·M.戴蒙德：《枪炮、病菌与钢铁：人类社会的命运》，纽约：W. W. 诺顿出版社，1999 年，第 399 页。

2. 戴蒙德：《枪炮、病菌与钢铁》，第 253 页。

3. 戴蒙德：《枪炮、病菌与钢铁》，第 410 页。

4. 戴蒙德：《枪炮、病菌与钢铁》，第 412 页。

5. 戴蒙德：《枪炮、病菌与钢铁》，第 413 页。

6. 戴蒙德：《枪炮、病菌与钢铁》，第 414 页。

7. 戴蒙德：《枪炮、病菌与钢铁》，第 414 页。

8. 戴蒙德：《枪炮、病菌与钢铁》，第 416 页。

9. 斯图尔特·维斯："行为分析学家眼中的世界历史：从贾雷德·戴蒙德《枪炮、病菌与钢铁》谈起"，《行为与社会学刊》第 11 卷，2001 年第 1 期，第 85 页。

10. 维斯："行为分析学家眼中的世界历史"，第 86 页。

11. 戴维·K.汉弗莱等："取消酒水销售时段限制对暴力行为的影响评估：间断时间序列研究"，《公共科学图书馆：综合》第 8 卷，2013 年第 2 期，第 1 页，登录日期 2015 年 7 月 15 日，doi:10.1371/journal.pone.0055581。

7 历史成就

要点 🔑

- 戴蒙德在《枪炮、病菌与钢铁》一书中提出的理论是最为严谨的世界历史理论之一。

- 一些评论家认为，戴蒙德所提出的不能算作真正的理论，而只是对现有权力格局的回溯研究。

- 评论界提出，戴蒙德书中谈到的某些已被欧洲人消灭的部落实际上并未消亡。

观点评价

　　贾雷德·戴蒙德在《枪炮、病菌与钢铁》一书中所提出的"宏大"理论是否具备说服力？这句话既"对"也"不对"。也许戴蒙德并没有推导出什么规律，他只是阐释了历史事实。旧世界征服了新世界，欧洲成为胜利者，似乎历史的发展只有一条路可走。历史作为一门学科是否适合用简约法 * 进行解释，路德维希·米塞斯研究所 * 的右翼经济学家吉恩·卡拉汉 * 提出了这一疑问[1]。

　　此处"简约法"的意思是把一系列复杂的事件归因于某一极为重要的因素。在《枪炮、病菌与钢铁》中，戴蒙德将人类历史的种种都归因于少数几个因素。卡拉汉提出，自然科学或许可以使用简约法阐释从高处掉落的苹果会自由落体坠下的问题，"但历史学家中却碰不到如此相似的案例"。[2]

　　历史学或其他社会科学是否存在定律仍有待商榷。假设历史有定律可循，那么戴蒙德的研究便是成功的。如果这一假设成立，那么便意味着从长远来看历史只能沿一条道路发展，其他道路决然不可能存在。但假若"历史"是一系列彼此之间会产生难以预测影响的单个事件串联而成的，那么《枪炮、病菌与钢铁》的宏大理论便不甚成立了。

> "虽然戴蒙德在书中提出了诸多洞见，但是这并不是他所认为的用科学方法重塑历史的第一步，不过是另一个审视人类历史的新奇角度。此外，他过度阐释的政治隐喻也不利于人类福祉和自由。"
>
> —— 吉恩·卡拉汉："戴蒙德的失误"

当时的成就

戴蒙德的《枪炮、病菌与钢铁》一书取得了极大的成功。1998年，这本书获得了普利策奖非虚构类作品奖，并被译为 36 种语言。在美国，国家地理学会还为此拍摄了电视纪录片，于 2005 年上映。此外，这本书还荣获 1997 年美国大学优等生荣誉学会科学图书奖，意在鼓励和支持戴蒙德提出的历史（及地理）也可真正被当作一门科学来研究的观点。

美国社会学家理查德·约克 * 和菲利普·曼库斯 * 在书评"璞玉之思"中分析了为何《枪炮、病菌与钢铁》会获得如此巨大的商业成就，却未能对环境社会学这门学科产生什么直接影响，特别是这本书还有着高度的科学性和严谨性。"这很讽刺，"他们说，"因为环境社会学……从根本上来说就是在研究人类社会如何受环境影响，又如何影响了环境。"[3]

戴蒙德采用简约法进行科学研究，是其学科影响力不足的原因之一。这与 20 世纪 90 年代早期社会科学中"文化转向"的研究热潮背道而驰。美国社会学家马克·雅各布斯 * 和林恩·斯皮尔曼 * 将其称之为上一代人文学科和社会科学中最具影响力的研究思潮之一。文化转向将社会科学视为探究特定语境下意义的工具，而非归纳出普适定律的手段。[4] 实际上，戴蒙德的观点与这一热潮并不相符。因此，他的著作在发展经济学领域拥有比在社会学领域更大的影响力。

局限性

美国人类学家迈克尔·威尔克斯 * 认为，许多人会发现《枪炮、病菌与钢铁》（以及随后出版的《大崩溃》）十分荒谬。威尔克斯认为，戴蒙德的疏漏在于那些自己声称已完全消亡的部落如美洲土著事实上并未消亡，尽管是以不同的形态而存在。他指出，戴蒙德所说的美洲土著部落已经"崩溃"的观点实则是一种普遍的误解，"大众对于征服与消亡的描述常常是一种错误的认知"。[5] 他问道："假如让考古学家来解释为什么哥伦布发现美洲后五百年的时间里那些原始部落依旧存在，而没有消失或被边缘化，他们会怎样作答呢？"[6]

威尔克斯认为，戴蒙德的"终极叙述"——面对殖民入侵，土著部落终会"消亡"——不仅准确性存疑，还会对现存的土著部落造成精神上的伤害。在"终极"叙述中，土著城市的"废址"被解释为社会崩溃的证据。威尔克斯反驳道，"另一种阐述的角度是站在土著部落的立场来看待那些考古遗址：将它们视作鲜活的宇宙与历史景观的一部分"，而这些地方目前依旧有土著居民居住。[7]

威尔克斯对《枪炮、病菌与钢铁》一书局限性的探讨深具远见：戴蒙德假定土著文化已经崩溃，现存的只是对过去的仿制，但是这一论点否定了尚未消亡的美国土著的存在。显然，美洲土著会拒绝这一观点。

1. 吉恩·卡拉汉："戴蒙德的失误"，米塞斯研究所，登录日期2015年5月17日，https://mises.org/library/diamond-fallacy。
2. 卡拉汉："戴蒙德的失误"。
3. 理查德·约克和菲利普·曼库斯："璞玉之思：论戴蒙德《枪炮、病菌与钢铁》"，《人类生态学研究》第14卷，2007年第2期，第157页。
4. 马克·D.雅各布斯和林恩·斯皮尔曼："学科分叉口上的文化社会学"，《诗学》第33卷，2005年，第1页。
5. 迈克尔·威尔克斯："市场征服及消失的印第安人：以原住民视角论贾雷德·戴蒙德的《枪炮、病菌与钢铁》"，《社会考古学》第10卷，2010第1期，第96页。
6. 迈克尔·威尔克斯：《印第安村庄的反抗和征服神话：印第安考古学研究》，伯克利：加利福尼亚大学出版社，2009年，第11页。
7. 威尔克斯：《印第安村庄的反抗》，第96页。

8 著作地位

要点 ⚙━

- 贾雷德·戴蒙德三本最著名的作品即《第三种黑猩猩》《枪炮、病菌与钢铁》和《大崩溃》，都是在探究那些驱动社会变革的最为重要的因素。

- 戴蒙德所有的著作都以严谨地运用比较法与"自然实验"而闻名。

- 《枪炮、病菌与钢铁》是戴蒙德最为出名的著作，屡获殊荣，并被翻译为 36 种语言。

定位

虽然让戴蒙德名声大噪的是非技术类图书，但他并不一直是畅销书作家。在《枪炮、病菌与钢铁》一书出版前，他所发表的多为专业期刊上的学术文章。

戴蒙德的第一本大众读物《第三种黑猩猩》出版于 1991 年。这本书与《枪炮、病菌与钢铁》一样，主要面向普通大众，而且探讨的也是人类如何主宰世界。在这本书中，戴蒙德意在寻找人类进化史中人类行为的种种根源。比如他注意到，在过去六万年的时间里，人类社会经历了"越进式发展"，其中包括贸易、文化及技术飞速发展和进步。这一现象发生于解剖学意义上的现代人类当中，戴蒙德认为这是人类能够开口讲话的结果。[1] 语言让人类可以"一起讨论如何改进生产工具，或交流刻在洞穴上的壁画意味着什么"[2]。

《枪炮、病菌与钢铁》之后，戴蒙德最为著名的作品是 2005

年出版的《大崩溃：社会如何选择兴亡》。《第三种黑猩猩》探讨的是人类进化，《枪炮、病菌与钢铁》探讨的是环境在人类社会发展中扮演的角色，《大崩溃》则探讨的是人类社会形成后发生了什么。所谓"崩溃"，戴蒙德指的是"长期以来，在相当广阔的区域中，人口和/或政治、社会、经济、社会复杂性的骤然减少"[3]。

> "当然，要说所有族群都将因自然环境破坏而走向灭亡，是不正确的：历史上有些族群灭亡了，有些则没有；真正的问题在于为何只有部分族群不堪一击，那些已经灭亡的和尚未灭亡的社会族群之间到底有何区别。"
>
> ——贾雷德·戴蒙德:《大崩溃》

整合

戴蒙德的著作，尤其是三部曲即《第三种黑猩猩》《枪炮、病菌与钢铁》和《大崩溃》都有一个特点，那就是采用了科学的研究方法。对戴蒙德而言，科学研究并不一定是在实验室环境下进行的试验，而是利用所有可能的方法"获取对世界的可靠认知"。[4] 此外，戴蒙德在其所有的著作中延续了同一个科学研究的目标：探究那些决定当今及未来世界面貌的**长期性**因素，包括生物学因素、环境因素和文化因素。

戴蒙德早期作品和《大崩溃》的关键区别之一是人类行为中结构（环境与制度的架构模式）与能动作用（自主选择）的重要性。《大崩溃》主要探讨人类的行为选择。戴蒙德写道，一些社会通过从经验中吸取教训、依据环境变化调整社会行为，成功解决了"极为棘手的环境问题"。方案可能是控制人口数量也可能是寻找新的食物来源或细化土地管理。[5] 这便是戴蒙德在书名中用"选择"一词的原因。

《大崩溃》与《枪炮、病菌与钢铁》尤其强调了这两个不同的因素（结构与能动作用）自史前时代以来对人类社会发展所产生的影响。《枪炮、病菌与钢铁》着力于阐释"建设"，而《大崩溃》则着力于解释另一种结局，即败落。从全局的角度来看待戴蒙德的作品，有助于展现从宏观视角——即宽阔的范围、长久的时间——阐释人类社会发展和理解普世规则的作用。

意义

戴蒙德在所有的著作中，都显示出了整合多个学科知识并将其普及给大众的能力。他赢得了广泛的追捧，其中包括多位公众人物如企业家、慈善家比尔·盖茨[*]，并在有关全球发展的讨论中具有一定影响力。随着《枪炮、病菌与钢铁》及其之后著作的出版，戴蒙德在人类历史和生态学领域亮出了独特、全面的观点，其国际声誉不断提升。

自《枪炮、病菌与钢铁》首次出版以来，更多与此书主题相关的新信息被披露，在戴蒙德看来，这些信息"丰富了我们的认知，但没有动摇最根本的理念"[6]。戴蒙德坚持自己的主要观点，认为各大陆板块自然环境的差异影响了人类历史的进程，相信书里的观点在如今全球发展的议题中仍然具有重要意义。

《枪炮、病菌与钢铁》令戴蒙德变得家喻户晓，至今仍是他作品中受到最广泛认可的一本书。世界各地的许多大学和高中课堂都将这本书列为现代经典阅读书目。

1. 贾雷德·戴蒙德:《第三种黑猩猩》,伦敦:温特吉出版社,2002年,第46页。

2. 戴蒙德:《第三种黑猩猩》,第47页。

3. 贾雷德·戴蒙德:《大崩溃:社会如何选择兴亡》,伦敦:企鹅出版社,2005年,第3页。

4. 戴蒙德:《大崩溃》,第17页。

5. 戴蒙德:《大崩溃》,第10页。

6. 贾雷德·戴蒙德:"枪炮、病菌与钢铁:人类社会的命运",登录日期2013年9月6日,http://www.jareddiamond.org/Jared_Diamond/Guns,_Germs,_and_Steel.html。

第三部分：学术影响

9 最初反响

要点 &

- 批评家们认为戴蒙德的观点是错误的，因为他的理论与整体假设都是在为欧洲殖民主义*的罪行"辩护"。

- 戴蒙德回应称历史学中的科学研究方法需要泛化。

- 戴蒙德和那些批评他的人代表了学术界相互对立的两派观点，对于学术应当做什么，应该是什么样子，以及科学性和严谨性的相对价值。

批评

贾雷德·戴蒙德的《枪炮、病菌与钢铁》一书因其许多欧洲中心主义*的假设（书中的论证都建立在欧洲占据主导地位的思想之上）而广受批评。

美国人类学家詹姆斯·布劳特*认为，这本书"颇具影响力的原因部分在于，对普通读者来说，欧洲中心主义的论调听起来十分有'科学'说服力。"[1] 布劳特的主要观点是，戴蒙德认为当今世界的发展格局注定无可避免，历史不可能沿其他道路发展；于是他一再努力地为这一事实辩护。从根本上来说，布劳特对戴蒙德的批评在于戴蒙德对欧洲而不是欧亚大陆在世界上占据统治地位的原因的解释。他指出技术的传播是欧亚大陆国家崛起的关键要素，之后欧洲才走上了全球统治地位。

"欧洲在差异过多和过少间保持了恰到好处的平衡"这一论点本身便存在问题，因为它意味着戴蒙德的论证是建立在回溯历史并为欧洲主导地位正名的基础上，他能够在"过多"与"过少"之间划分出一条界线。[2] 从本质上来讲，布劳特对《枪炮、病菌与钢铁》一书的批评是，戴蒙德并未从真正意义上努力尝试探究出一种可以预测社会发展结果的理论，而只是对当今世界权力分配的现状进行阐释，使其看起来像是"自然发展"的结果。

人类学家弗雷德里克·埃林顿*和黛博拉·吉沃茨*在 2004 年合著的《耶利之问》中直接回应了戴蒙德的作品。这本书以新几内亚政治家耶利向贾雷德·戴蒙德提出的问题命名："为什么你们白人制造了那么多的货物并把它们运到新几内亚来，而我们黑人却几乎没有属于我们自己的货物呢？"[3] "我们认为戴蒙德的观点很有问题，"他们写道，"深入理解历史的宏大进程，竟可以不去考虑人类生活的现状和未来。"[4] 换句话说，埃林顿和吉沃茨认为，戴蒙德误解了耶利所提出的问题。耶利的兴趣点并不在西方人发明的那些伟大创造上，而是"西方世界的傲慢竟导致欧洲人否定巴布亚新几内亚的基本价值"。[5] 也就是说，耶利在质疑为何西方人手握权力而新几内亚人（及其他发展中国家的民众）却长期处于劣势。从这一角度来看，戴蒙德的回答更像是在找借口而不是对此进行解释，西方人注定会征服世界，而当今世界局势是地理环境差异所造成的不可避免的结果。[6]

最后，埃林顿和吉沃茨反对能动作用这一观点：我们不能仅仅因为某一社会发明了枪炮与钢铁，就判定他们会一直处于霸主地位。这种假定先入为主地把所有人视为利己和贪婪的，但并非每个人的本性都如此。他们写道："欧洲人拥有资源，总是傲慢地对待耶利和其他巴布亚新几内亚人。"但是不能仅仅因为西方人有此能力，就宽恕他们的行为。[7] 也就是说，个人的选择必须放到大环境中进行考量。

> "我不同意戴蒙德的观点，不是因为他试图用科学数据与科学推理去解决人类历史的问题。这种研究方法本身值得赞扬推广。但是，他在没有找到合理答案的情况下，宣称自己的研究成果切实可靠且有科学依据，完全忽视社会科学的研究成果、一味鼓吹过时且不可信的环境决定论，那这就一定是伪科学。"
>
> —— 詹姆斯·布劳特："环境保护主义与欧洲中心主义"

回应

戴蒙德对这些批评回应道，他们误解了自己的立场，"我们的分歧源于所考量的历史范畴不同"。[8] 从本质上来说，批评戴蒙德的人认为，他的理论中没有给文化和民族自决留以足够空间。对此他的回应是，文化所能决定的具体范围是由漫长的历史进程决定的。在谈及结束于 12 000 年前的最后一次冰河时期*时，他写道："综观后冰河时期数百代人的历史，以及广袤大陆上数千个社会族群，文化差异很难成为解决自然环境局限的途径。"[9] 戴蒙德已经尽可能从最广阔的视角着手书写历史。因此，他需要做出一些假设，将个人在历史中所起的作用一再淡化，不过他也因此得以总结出人类历史发展的普适规律。

戴蒙德认为，批评者所提出的研究方法可以用于回答发生于特定时间的特定事件的一些具体问题。想要知晓第二次世界大战发生的时间、地点及缘由，就不能不去探究德国与欧洲其他国家的具体关系及《凡尔赛条约》*。但是，若问及涵盖面广泛的宏观问题，例如"相比世界其他地区，为何第二次世界大战期间欧洲的工业发展遥遥领先？"，便需要一套在最大范畴内普遍适用的理论来解答。

冲突与共识

在这场争论中，戴蒙德与批评者都没有改变自身的立场；对于学术应当做什么，应该是什么样子，他们的观点有着本质的分歧。事实上，戴蒙德认为学术研究的任务是客观公正地呈现 13 000 年以来的人类历史。这意味着他拒绝从能动因素作用（在这一作用下，社会的发展被视为不同族群独立选择的体现）的角度进行阐释，该因素并不一定是以对结构的适应度为标准来"评估"社会。批评戴蒙德的人如埃林顿和吉沃茨，认为他不重视那些未能主宰世界的族群，即便这些社会的存在代表着生活在其中的民众对自身文化的偏好（比如狩猎采集部落也许十分珍视他们的生活方式，并不认为自己不走运或失败）。

这一争论在戴蒙德最新的作品《昨日之前的世界》中仍有体现。他在这本书里写道："传统社会族群代表着数千个长达千年的组织了人类生活方式的自然实验"[10]。加拿大人类学家韦德·戴维斯 * 在评论这本书时提出了自己的批评，戴蒙德无法接受人类发展的多样化；他写道，"世界上其他族群未步入现代化并非失败，未能成为同我们一样的社会更不是什么失败。"[11] 换句话说，消亡或被吞并的部落，在戴蒙德和戴维斯这样的理论家眼中是截然不同的两种结果。在戴蒙德看来，他们代表着行不通的失败做法；而在戴维斯看来，他们是那个时代、那个地方人们身份的独特体现。这两种观点都是正确的。但其根本出发点迥异，且互不相容。

1. 詹姆斯·布劳特："环境保护论与欧洲中心主义",《地理评论》第89卷,1999年第3期,第403页。

2. 布劳特："环境保护论与欧洲中心主义",第403页。

3. 贾雷德·M.戴蒙德:《枪炮、病菌与钢铁:人类社会的命运》,纽约:W. W. 诺顿出版社,1999年,第14页。

4. 弗雷德里克·埃林顿和黛博拉·吉沃茨:《耶利之问:糖、文化与历史》,芝加哥:芝加哥大学出版社,2004年,第7页。

5. 埃林顿和吉沃茨:《耶利之问》,第8页。

6. 埃林顿和吉沃茨:《耶利之问》,第9页。

7. 埃林顿和吉沃茨:《耶利之问》,第14页。

8. 贾雷德·戴蒙德:"枪炮、病菌与钢铁",《纽约书评》,1997年6月26日,登录日期2015年5月23日,http://www.nybooks.com/articles/archives/1997/jun/26/guns-germs-and-steel/。

9. 戴蒙德:"枪炮、病菌与钢铁"。

10. 贾雷德·戴蒙德:《昨日之前的世界:我们能从传统社会学到什么?》,伦敦:企鹅出版社,2013年,第32页。

11. 韦德·戴维斯:"论贾雷德·戴蒙德《昨日之前的世界》",《卫报》,2013年1月9日,登录日期2015年5月23日,http://www.theguardian.com/books/2013/jan/09/history-society。

10 后续争议

要点 🔑

- 发展经济学旨在探究经济发展的规律与原理,《枪炮、病菌与钢铁》一书已成为发展经济学研究的一部分。

- 发展经济学将一国的自然资源优势与其取得经济成功的可能性联系在一起。

- 美国经济学家杰弗里·萨克斯 * 的著作,可能是这一学派最有影响力的作品,特别是他所提出的"资源诅咒"概念。

应用与问题

地理学、政治学和经济学(特别是发展经济学)领域的纷争,提及了戴蒙德在《枪炮、病菌与钢铁》中所提出的一些观点,即便只是含蓄地提了一下。一方面,学术界有"经验主义"或"实证主义"的主流研究方法;这种方法注重研究的科学性,利用已有数据和技术信息,进行总结和概括,世界银行 * 等机构常常会采用这种研究方法[1]。另一方面,侧重于探讨思想和义化影响的研究方法则不在主流之内。他们提出,更多的"科学"理论在隐晦地为发达世界凌驾于发展中世界之上做辩护,同时在"不知不觉间寄希望于一套固执的话语,指出需要做出改变的是**发展中国家**,而不是**发达国家**"。[2]

例如,戴蒙德 2005 年出版的《大崩溃》一书与联合国重要文件《2005 年世界资源报告》有不少重要的相似之处。"很久前便有预测,"戴蒙德写道,"(社会崩溃的原因是)人们不经意间(破坏）了社会赖以生存的自然资源。"[3] 他提出，导致社会崩溃的自然环境问题有"砍伐森林、栖息地破坏、土壤问题……水资源管理问题……过度狩猎、过度捕捞、外来物种入侵、人口数量增长以及日益增加的人均需求"[4]。

实际上，人类在与自然环境相处的过程中犯了许多错。《世界资源报告》开篇便提出"生态系统代表着地球的自然资本存量"，"在过去50年里，为了满足对食品、淡水、木材和纤维制品日益增长的需求，我们对生态环境的改变比人类历史上任何时期都要快得多"[5]。报告提出："为了满足长期稳定的生产率，便出现了对生态系统疏于管理的情况"[6]。自然环境与政治、经济发展息息相关以及问题的判断和解决有"一个正确答案"的观点，与戴蒙德的分析不谋而合，而且仍然具有重要意义。

> "贫人可以通过从生态系统中攫取更大的利益来改善生活。但这种情况发生的前提是有良好的监管措施，即一方面保持生态系统可持续发展，另一方面确保穷人的利益、发言权与参与。也就是说，生态系统本身就有助于扶贫减贫，但只有当我们合理有效地利用这种力量，对资源进行监管，穷人才能从中获益。"
>
> —— 格雷戈里·莫克：《世界资源报告》

思想流派

戴蒙德的著作对明确发展经济学家长期以来所探讨的问题发挥了重要作用。

发展经济学家保罗·斯特里坦*在其1971年发表的一篇文章里概述了这一问题。关于欠发达问题最显著的事实是，欠发达国家"位于热带气候*和亚热带地区",而考虑这一点是否为巧合让这一问题变得更加复杂。他提出不发达国家在"解决发展问题时带有根深蒂固的乐观偏差,而且不情愿承认原始环境存在巨大的差异"。[7]

同时,美国经济学家戴维·兰德斯列举了多种导致不均衡发展的自然环境条件;他强调高温会导致传染疾病增多,使劳动更加困难。[8]

发展经济学领域认同戴蒙德有关地理与经济发展关系的观点最为重要的著作之一,便是经济学家约翰·盖洛普*、杰弗里·萨克斯和安德鲁·梅林格*的作品。他们考察了世界上所有国家的地理位置和政治历史(比如,这些国家的统治者是否为独裁者),还有各个国家的平均收入。结果发现"拥有最适宜地理与政治条件的23个国家,它们位于北半球,是温带气候*且沿海,未受战争摧残,平均(收入)为18 000美元"[9]。而位于南半球热带地区的内陆国家以及其他条件相似的国家,平均收入却会因环境而减少几万美元。[10]

当代研究

自然环境对人类社会的发展有重要影响。如今认同戴蒙德这一观点的重要思想家当属经济学家杰弗里·萨克斯。萨克斯在文章《制度重要,却不决定所有》中指出,人类因素(广义上被定义为"制度",包含从传统到政府的一切)只是经济发展影响因素的一部分。萨克斯把自己的观点与环境决定论*(即在发展问题上,自然环境条件决定一切)区别开来,提出即便良好的健康"对发展至关重要",因气候要素而导致疟疾*高发的地区会遇到特殊困难，但这并不意味着该地区注定永远贫困。[11] 萨克斯得出结论，自然环境决定了国家在发展过程中所遇到的特定挑战。将所有问题归咎于"糟糕的制度"或富国对穷国的剥削，就是在忽视这些重要的环境因素。[12]

萨克斯（以及美国经济学家安德鲁·沃纳＊）眼中最为重要的环境因素之一，是所谓的"资源诅咒"，指拥有丰富自然资源的国家本可以取得经济繁荣，却发展滞后，或最终管理不当、出现严峻社会问题的现象。资源诅咒**如何**阻碍发展，这一问题仍无明确定论，但萨克斯和沃纳的一个观点是，虽然采掘、售卖丰沃的自然资源可能会带来财富，但却不能给国家带来更为广阔的经济发展前景。[13] 也就是说，拥有石油资源的国家可以与海外石油企业合作出售石油，却未能借此优势发展本国工业。而当石油资源枯竭，本国就会几乎无实业（出口高价值工业制品的产业）可依，作为石油产业的替代。

与戴蒙德不同，萨克斯无意研究 13 000 年来历史发展的结果，但他们有一个重要的共同关注点，那就是自然环境对社会选择的影响与限制。

---

1. 莫林·希基和维基·劳森："超越科学？人类地理学、阐释和批评"，《地理学质疑：百家争鸣》，诺埃尔·卡斯特里等编，马萨诸塞州莫尔登：布莱克威尔出版社，2005 年，第 110 页。

2. 希基和劳森："超越科学？"，第 109 页。

3. 贾雷德·M.戴蒙德：《大崩溃：社会如何选择兴亡》，伦敦：企鹅出版社，2005

年，第 4 页。

4. 戴蒙德：《大崩溃》，第 4 页。

5. 格雷戈里·默克编：《2005 年世界资源报告》，华盛顿：世界资源研究所，2005
  年，第 4 页。

6. 默克：《2005 年世界资源报告》，第 7 页。

7. 保罗·斯特里坦："穷国有多穷？"，《分化世界的发展》，D. 希尔斯和 L. 乔伊
  编，哈默兹沃思：企鹅出版社，1971 年，第 78 页。

8. 戴维·兰德斯：《国富国穷：为什么有的国家如此富有而有的国家如此贫穷》，
  纽约：W. W. 诺顿出版社，1998 年，第 7—11 页。

9. 约翰·盖洛普等：《地理学与经济发展》，剑桥：国家经济研究局，1998 年，第
  8 页。

10. 盖洛普等：《地理学与经济发展》，第 8 页。

11. 杰弗里·萨克斯："制度重要，但并非万能"，《经济与发展》第 40 卷，2003 年
  6 月第 2 期，第 40 页。

12. 萨克斯："制度重要，但并非万能"，第 38—39 页。

13. 杰弗瑞·萨克斯和安德鲁·沃纳："自然资源诅咒"，《欧洲经济评论》第 45
  卷，2001 年第 4—6 期，第 833 页。

11 当代印迹

要点 🔑

- 如今，比起其他采用相同科学研究方法的著作（特别是发展经济学领域），《枪炮、病菌与钢铁》影响力相对较小。

- 例如，加拿大经济学家南森·纳恩*提出，非洲某些区域被贩卖奴隶的数量与其当下的欠发达水平有紧密联系。

- 批评这一研究方法的学者认为，该方法过于简化，忽视了许多复杂的因素，如统治权力的关联，这一因素比任何"潜在"因素都更能起到决定作用。

地位

贾雷德·戴蒙德的《枪炮、病菌与钢铁》一书在国际史、政治学、经济学、地理学、社会学等多个学科的本科生阅读书目中占据重要地位。部分原因是这本书文笔流畅、影响广泛且通俗易懂。

然而从学术角度来讲，这本书的科学性有所欠缺。例如美国历史学家斯蒂芬·韦特海姆*在对《昨日之前的世界》的书评中写道："《枪炮、病菌与钢铁》抨击了种族优势决定西方统治地位的观念，而这个观点几乎没有什么重要学者会当真并做研究。"[1] 经济学家德隆·阿西莫格鲁*和詹姆斯·罗宾逊*的重要著作《国家为什么会失败》则提出了更为温和的观点：《枪炮、病菌与钢铁》之所以"不能被用于解释现代世界的不公平"，是因为它太过简化，这也就意味着它无法解释为何"普通西班牙人的平均收入会比普通秘鲁人高出六倍多"，以及怎样纠正这样的状况。[2]

《枪炮、病菌与钢铁》在当今的重要性更在于它在最大范围内使用了"比较研究法"（通过分析两个或两个以上案例的相似与差异之处探究既定因素对已有结果的影响的方法）。在戴蒙德和英国政治理论家詹姆斯·罗宾逊合作编著的《历史的自然实验》中，戴蒙德拓展了这一观点，并探究了其运用的多种可能。"历史比较法，"书中总结道，"能够得出研究单个案例无法得出的结论"，而且"当一个案例推导出结论时，另一个案例可［通过实证证据］来强化结论"。[3]

那么，为何《枪炮、病菌与钢铁》在如今仍有重要意义？部分原因是它向本科学生以深入浅出、通俗易懂的方式，介绍了比较研究法。正如我们所看到的，也许如今它在学术界依旧被广泛研读，是因为它的研究方法，而非它的结论与观点。

> "相比墨西哥和拉丁美洲的其他国家，为何美国的制度更有助于推动经济发展？这个问题的答案在于殖民早期所形成的不同类型的社会。制度差异从那时起便开始存在，其影响一直延续到今天。要理解这一差异，我们的研究必须追溯至北美及拉丁美洲殖民地建立之初。"
>
> —— 德隆·阿西莫格鲁和詹姆斯·罗宾逊：《国家为什么会失败》

互动

如今，戴蒙德和其他历史学家所提出的挑战，更倾向于聚焦文化人类学和科学之间的区别。

比如，在戴蒙德与罗宾逊合作编著的《历史的自然实验》一书中，经济学家南森·纳恩写了其中一个章节"历史的镣铐：非洲奴隶贸易的起因与影响"。在这一章节中，纳恩发现"那些过去被贩卖奴隶人数最多的地区，正是如今最为贫困的地区"[4]。纳恩的发现最为让人印象深刻的是其科学的严谨性；纳恩"通过分析数据，探讨了非洲不同地区奴隶贸易现象的严重程度与随之而来的经济表现之间的关系"[5]。他对非洲奴隶贸易的分析建立在广阔的视角之上，例如他将现代的津巴布韦和刚果所在的两块区域的际遇当作类似的案例进行比较，从而得出综合性结论。

在普遍性与特殊性之间找到平衡，是一项很艰巨的挑战。不论是谁都会认同，不同地区奴隶贸易状况各不相同。但纳恩所进行的自然实验能够呈现出几个共同因素，如奴隶贸易的严重程度；这些对于阐释不同族群当下的境遇有重要作用。

持续争议

美国人类学家帕特里夏·麦克纳尼*和诺曼·约菲*合著的《崩溃之问》一书提出了一系列对戴蒙德观点的评论。

与此同时，美国人类学家弗雷德里克·埃林顿和黛博拉·吉沃茨进一步完善了他们在批评戴蒙德《枪炮、病菌与钢铁》的著作《耶利之问》中的观点，在"在历史叙述中为既得利益群体开脱并指责弱势群体"一文中提出了新的论点。他们指出戴蒙德"将历史置于看似是共识的（西方的）推测之上，将复杂的政治进程转化为必然发生的简单定律"。将历史基于"定律"，从而令当下的时局看起来像是自然发生的一切。[6]

他们指出，问题在于以此观点看待历史，便会认为西班牙征服者的野蛮行径并无道德上的差错。人为不可控制的因素（即欧亚大陆的地理特征与动植物的分布情况）意味着，西班牙人对他国的殖民是不由自主的行为，而安迪斯山脉的居民则从一开始便注定了被殖民的命运。这一观点反驳了贯穿于《大崩溃》与《枪炮、病菌与钢铁》两本书的主题。他们指出，戴蒙德在《大崩溃》中假定，从文化因素，到抵御外部势力的暴行，再到单纯的厄运，每一社会族群"都有平等的选择权"。这样的假设"令我们在理解世界历史时面临重重困惑"。[7]

埃林顿和吉沃茨以美国和巴布亚新几内亚的制糖产业为例阐明观点。美国给本国的制糖产业提供补贴*（用公款补贴，确保本国生产的白糖在开放市场上价格低廉）。而另一方面，"巴布亚新几内亚政府却由于受到来自世界银行和世界贸易组织*的压力"，在开放市场上缺乏竞争力。[8] 这意味着他们既不能补贴本国的制糖产业，又无法对美国白糖征收进口税费（即"关税"）。我们不清楚这样的局面如何会是巴布亚新几内亚政府的自主选择，更不清楚美国国际贸易强国的地位如何因历史必然性而变得顺理成章。

---

1. 斯蒂芬·韦特海姆："追寻者的喋喋不休"，《国家》，2013 年 4 月 22 日，第 37 页。
2. 德隆·阿西莫格鲁和詹姆斯·罗宾逊：《国家为什么会失败：权力、富裕与贫困的根源》，伦敦：档案出版社，2012 年，第 52 页。
3. 贾雷德·戴蒙德和詹姆斯·罗宾逊："后记"，《历史的自然实验》，贾雷德·戴蒙德和詹姆斯·罗宾逊编，马萨诸塞州坎布里奇：哈佛大学出版社，2010 年，第 274 页。
4. 南森·纳恩："历史的镣铐：非洲奴隶贸易的起因与影响"，《历史的自然实验》，贾雷德·戴蒙德和詹姆斯·罗宾逊编，马萨诸塞州坎布里奇：哈佛大学出版社，2010 年，第 142 页。

5. 纳恩："历史的镣铐"，第 146 页。

6. 弗雷德里克·埃林顿和黛博拉·吉沃茨："历史叙述对利益既得者的袒护与对未得者的谴责"，《崩溃之问：人类适应性、生态脆弱性和帝国余波》，帕特里夏·麦克纳尼和诺曼·约菲编，剑桥：剑桥大学出版社，2009 年，第 329—351、330 页。

7. 埃林顿和吉沃茨："对利益既得者的袒护"，第 341 页。

8. 埃林顿和吉沃茨："对利益既得者的袒护"，第 348—349 页。

12 未来展望

要点 🔑

- 《枪炮、病菌与钢铁》巩固了戴蒙德公共知识分子的名声,他也将书中所采用的研究方法应用到当代其他问题的研究中。

- 戴蒙德关注更多的是文化和方法论,而英裔美国历史学者伊恩·莫里斯 * 则担当起了阐释长时段历史 * 的任务。

- 《枪炮、病菌与钢铁》为国际发展不平衡这一棘手问题提供了严谨而又科学的解答。

潜力

贾雷德·戴蒙德《枪炮、病菌与钢铁》一书自身的影响力似乎并没有延续下去,其他人类学家或社会学家大多没有将戴蒙德的论点纳为正统,他们认为戴蒙德不论是在实证方面,还是在将历史作为科学来研究的整体目标方面,都存在差错。但是在历史领域中《枪炮、病菌与钢铁》确实在普及比较研究法方面大有贡献。

戴蒙德近来出版的有关发展经济学的作品,探讨了较短时间范畴内更为具体的问题,在学界仍旧占有重要的地位。面对美国全球影响力逐渐下降、财政预算压力攀升的现状,戴蒙德在近期的一篇文章中提出了这样一个问题:"美国将走向何方?"[1]

戴蒙德重申了自己的观点,政治上的竞争能够推动思想和社会的发展,并淘汰错误的思想(如废除海军、瓦解中产阶层等)。[2]

戴蒙德指出了美国面临的四大威胁:政治妥协概率的下降;选举权的限制日益增多;贫富差距日益扩大;智慧资本 *(国家在思

想、技术和创新方面拥有的财富）发展机遇减少。[3] 戴蒙德认为，这意味着美国将渐渐失去长久积累起来的种种竞争优势。

> "长时段研究和短时段研究一致承认，过去两百年来西方占据世界统治地位，但对两百年之前的历史有所分歧。产生分歧的原因在于他们对前现代历史的假定不同。解决这个分歧唯一的办法是，将研究范围推进至更早的时期，从而构建起'总体'的历史样貌。"
>
> —— 伊恩·莫里斯：《西方将主宰多久》

未来方向

戴蒙德又写了几部书，探讨文化（《昨日之前的世界》）和研究方法（《历史的自然实验》）。但传统历史学家伊恩·莫里斯最近出版的两本书将《枪炮、病菌与钢铁》中的假设推到学界视野的前沿。

他的书《西方将主宰多久：从历史的发展模式看世界的未来》（2010）尝试在全球历史研究领域建立起长时段和短时段研究间的桥梁。莫里斯写道："如果我们把研究视野限制在史前时期或是现代，我们将无法找到答案。"相反，历史学家应当"将浩瀚的人类历史视作统一的整体，呈现历史完整的原貌"。[4] 戴蒙德认为只有最早期的因素才能作为起因（其余的只是后续的连锁反应），而莫里斯则相信"根本"原因能够从历史长河中不断产生。他指出："西方的主宰既不是源于数千年前就已注定的优势，也不是近来诸多历史事件所造成的后果。"[5]

莫里斯这本书的核心观念是"社会发展"，他将这一概念解释为"一个族群利用自然环境与智慧环境把'事情做好'的能力……

达成技术、农业、管理和文化方面的成就",以此理解和管理自然和社会。[6]

莫里斯得出结论,认为地理和"社会发展"决定了历史的样貌,且不断重新定义彼此,"地理因素决定了哪里的社会发展将迅速崛起,而崛起社会的发展则改变了地理因素所带来的影响"。[7]中世纪以后,欧洲国家技术迅速发展,英国或许因为是个远离大陆的岛国而落于其后,但当拥有强大的海军对称霸世界至关重要的时候,英国位于大西洋的地理位置便成了其发展帝国的重要优势。

小结

贾雷德·戴蒙德的《枪炮、病菌与钢铁》是一部颇具现实意义与争议的著作。世界为何会是今天的格局,特别是"西方"为何会如此强大,戴蒙德对这一问题的解答,意在超越简单的、显而易见的答案。他抛却了那些只看到显性"直接"原因(即将西方占据统治地位的原因归于强大的技术或是单一的管理模式)的答案,因为这些并不是全部的真相。他希望更加深入地挖掘,找到"根本"原因:假如技术发展是走向世界统治地位的关键,那么为何西方在当时能发展出更为先进的技术呢?

为了回答这一问题,戴蒙德转向考古学,来审视族群间最初的差异:因技术发展而演进为复杂社会的族群和未发展出复杂技术仍停留在狩猎采集社会的族群。他们之间最重要的区别在于**农业**。步入农业社会的族群,有足够能力供养专职的统治者、科学家、匠人和抄写员。为了寻找最为根本的原因,戴蒙德又继续深挖:为何有些族群步入了农业社会,而其他族群则没有?自然界随机的地理因素决定了适合驯化的动植物的分布情况。在戴蒙德看来，这会不可避免地引导族群走向农业社会，形成复杂社会，走向"枪炮、病菌与钢铁"，并最终让西方国家走上世界统治地位。

1. 贾雷德·戴蒙德："美国民主面临的四大威胁"，《治理》第 27 卷，2014 年第 2 期，第 189 页。

2. 戴蒙德："美国民主面临的四大威胁"，第 186 页。

3. 戴蒙德："美国民主面临的四大威胁"，第 186—187 页。

4. 伊恩·莫里斯：《西方将主宰多久：从历史的发展模式看世界的未来》，纽约：法勒、施特劳斯和吉鲁出版社，2010 年，第 22 页。

5. 莫里斯：《西方将主宰多久》，第 25 页。

6. 莫里斯：《西方将主宰多久》，第 144 页。

7. 莫里斯：《西方将主宰多久》，第 35 页。

术语表

1. **年鉴学派**：一个强调影响日常生活的是长期因素而非重大事件的历史学派。

2. **卡哈马卡**：秘鲁的一个主要城市。也是当时西班牙征服者和南美印加人爆发战争的地方。

3. **资本主义**：一种由私人掌管大多数（但不一定是全部）工业活动以获取利益的经济体系。

4. **冷战**（1947—1991）：美国和苏联及其各自的盟国间对峙紧张的时期。这两大阵营从未爆发过正面的军事冲突，而是进行边缘战争和间谍活动。

5. **殖民主义**：中心国家入侵并在目标领土建立殖民地的行为，特征是殖民者与本土居民之间极不平等的关系。

6. **比较研究法**：分析两个案例，并指出导致二者不同结果的深层原因。

7. **西班牙征服者**：指15至17世纪间，在"发现"新大陆的同时，征服美洲、大洋洲甚至亚洲部分地区的西班牙和葡萄牙探险者及军队。

8. **专制**：一种权力集中于一人或一群人手中的政府形式。

9. **驯化**：人类通过选择性育种培育或淘汰生物某些特征，以使其更加适合人类社会的需要。

10. **经验主义**：一种知识理论。该理论认为知识只能来源于一个人所观察到的东西。

11. **环境决定论**：自然环境因素"锁定"既有历史轨迹的一种理论。该理论否认能动作用（个人可以通过行动改变社会）的力量，是结构主义的极端形式。

12. **欧洲中心主义**：对许多西方社会科学理论的一种批判。西方学界许多理论的假设是对欧洲人有利的，特别是认为欧洲及欧洲的思想拥有天然的优越性，而在其他文化看来，这一切并不是顺理成章的。

13. **全球化**：随着旅行、船运和电信等技术的完善，世界各地联系日益密切的过程。

14. **狩猎—采集社会**：指依靠野外食物（即靠狩猎而非蓄养家畜，靠采摘植物果实而非种植农作物）生存的人类小群体。这些社会通常频繁迁徙，且需要在食物采集上花费大量时间。

15. **冰河时期**：指地球表面温度下降的漫长时期。在冰河时期中，北美及欧洲大部分地区将被冰川冰所覆盖。上一个冰河时期距今 12 500 年。

16. **智慧资本**：指思想、知识和创新的价值。

17. **实验室环境**：指精密控制下的实验室环境，在此环境下可以不受外部世界干扰而得出最精确的研究结论。

18. **长时段**：法语短语，意为"长期"，指在历史学语境下年鉴学派所使用的一种研究方法，将历史变革（常常是社会变革）置于长期的历史中进行考量。

19. **路德维希·冯·米塞斯研究所**：指来自美国的一个智库，提倡政府减少对日常生活的干涉。该研究所以奥地利经济学家路德维希·冯·米塞斯的名字命名，路德维希认为政府的干预规划远不如自由市场有效率。

20. **疟疾**：一种由蚊子携带的寄生虫所引起的传染病，只出现在气候温暖潮湿的地区。2010 年有 60 多万人死于疟疾。

21. **人地关系地理学**：地理学四大研究传统之一，关注环境与人类之间如何互相影响。

22. **自然实验**：需要有两组大体相似的群体暴露在不同的环境中，这种情况多出于偶然。研究者可由此观察比较出不同的环境对群体有何影响。

23. **自然选择**：由查尔斯·达尔文首次提出，指既定环境下生物特征会对繁殖顺利与否产生影响，进而导致这些特征被保留或被淘汰。

24. **简约法**：指理论预测应当尽可能简化，最低限度地使用必要系数的原则。

25. **过程主义考古学**：考古学的一个思想流派，认为考古研究应当运用历史的物证来还原真实的历史，旨在以文化间的共性为基础总结出人类行为的某些"定律"。

26. **普利策奖**：美国一项表彰报纸、网络新闻、文学和音乐创作方面取得成就者的极有声誉的奖项。

27. **石器时代**：包含两种不同但有所关联的意思。一是公元前 6000 年至公元前 3000 年人类使用石器工具的史前时期。二是一些散落分布的狩猎—采集部落至今仍所处的技术发展阶段。

28. **结构主义**：社会科学领域看待世界的一种方式，强调外部环境对人类行为的塑造作用。该理论反对人的能动作用，而能动作用关注的是个体动机所起到的作用。

29. **补贴**：指对某一经济领域进行的财政支持（通常由政府提供），旨在让这一领域在市场上获得更大的竞争力。

30. **温带气候**：位于温暖的热带与寒冷的极地地区之间，温带气候四季分明，气候温和。

31. **《凡尔赛条约》**（1919）：指第一次世界大战结束后协约国与战败国德国签订的和平条约，因其对德国处罚过重让德国脆弱的经济雪上加霜而在历史上备受指责。

32. **热带气候**：位于赤道附近，常年温暖。

33. **欠发达**：指未充分利用资源发挥其生产潜力的国家的经济发展状况。

34. **不均衡发展**：指不同地区经济发展状况不平衡的状态。

35. **联合国**：一个由世界各国政府（几乎囊括所有的国家）组成的超国家组织，总部位于纽约，致力于维护国际安全、促进全球合作。

36. **世界银行**：总部位于华盛顿哥伦比亚特区的国际组织，为需要发展援助的国家提供贷款与咨询。

37. **世界体系论**：一种世界社会学与历史学研究理论，指出一些边缘国家受到中心国家系统性的剥削。

38. **世界贸易组织**：总部位于瑞士日内瓦的国际组织，负责管理国际贸易，维护贸易的公平与开放。

39. **第二次世界大战**（1939—1945）：轴心国（德国、意大利、日本）与取得胜利的同盟国（英国及其殖民地、自治领、苏联、美国）之间爆发的世界性战争。

人名表

1. 德隆·阿西莫格鲁（1967 年生），土耳其裔美国发展经济学家。他与经济学家詹姆斯·罗宾逊都从"制度"的角度研究发展问题，认为拥有"良好"（不压榨、公正等特质的）制度的国家社会发展要优于制度"糟糕"的国家。

2. 阿塔瓦尔帕（1500—1533），印加帝国统治者。1532 年阿塔瓦尔帕被西班牙人俘虏，短暂囚禁后被处死。

3. 詹姆斯·布劳特（1927—2000），伊利诺伊大学芝加哥分校人类学教授，主要贡献在于指出主流历史研究中所存在的欧洲中心主义偏见。

4. 费尔南·布罗代尔（1902—1985），法国历史学家，年鉴学派代表学者，主张在研究推动历史发展的因素时，应关注大范围的、长期的社会经济变迁，而非帝王的决定。

5. 吉恩·卡拉汉（1959 年生），美国经济学家。卡拉汉认为经济发展依靠自由市场，而非中央计划。

6. 威廉·卡顿（1929—2015），美国社会学家，环境社会学创始者之一，该学科是首个提出以超越社会因素视角进行研究的社会学分支学科。

7. 克里斯托弗·哥伦布（1451—1506），意大利探险家。为寻找到达印度的新航线，从欧洲启航，穿越大西洋，于 1942 年抵达美洲大陆。

8. 艾尔弗雷德·克罗斯比（1931—2018），美国历史学家、地理学家。代表作《哥伦布大交换》探讨了 1492 年哥伦布旅行后世界两大曾经分隔的主要陆地板块突然相互联系所产生的影响。

9. 查尔斯·达尔文（1809—1882），英国博物学家，提出了著名的"自然选择进化论"。

10. 韦德·戴维斯（1953 年生），加拿大人类学家、博物学家。他的著作强调不同文化间的差异，反对文化存在高下之分的理论。

11. **赖利·邓拉普**，美国俄克拉荷马州立大学社会学教授。与威廉·卡顿一样，邓拉普也以提出环境社会学理论而闻名。

12. **弗雷德里克·埃林顿**，康涅狄格州三一学院著名人类学教授。他在与黛博拉·吉沃茨合著的书中，强调经济与文化的主题、复杂的变革理论和多视角研究的重要性。

13. **约翰·盖洛普**（1962 年生），美国发展经济学家。他已发表多篇论文，阐述不同地理因素对社会发展结果的影响。

14. **比尔·盖茨**（1955 年生），美国企业家、慈善家，曾多年蝉联世界首富宝座。他创立了微软公司，并赚得巨额财富，现致力于通过比尔及梅琳达·盖茨基金会支持各地的经济发展。

15. **黛博拉·吉沃茨**，马萨诸塞州阿莫斯特学院人类学教授。她在与弗雷德里克·埃林顿合著的书籍中，强调了经济与文化的主题、复杂的变革理论和多视角研究的重要性。

16. **戴维·汉弗莱**，英国牛津大学格林坦普顿学院社会政策学教授。

17. **埃尔斯沃思·亨廷顿**（1876—1947），美国地理学家。著名的地理环境决定论就是由他提出。

18. **马克·D. 雅各布斯**，美国乔治梅森大学社会学教授。他的主要研究方向是社会学学科发展趋势以及金融社会学。

19. **埃里克·琼斯**（1936 年生），英裔澳大利亚经济历史学家。他的著作《欧洲奇迹》旨在分析欧洲工业生产力水平领先世界的原因。

20. **戴维·兰德斯**（1924—2013），美国哈佛大学经济与历史学教授。

21. **菲利普·曼库斯**，美国红杉学院心理学与社会学教授。他的主要研究方向为人类行为。

22. **帕特里夏·麦克纳尼**（1963 年生），美国人类学家，主要研究美洲玛雅文明的历史及考古。

23. **安德鲁·梅林格**，美国经济学家，已出版多部知名著作探讨发展经济学与地理学之间的关系。

24. **伊恩·莫里斯**（1960 年生），英裔美国历史学家，古典历史专家，主要研究长时段历史，近期发表的作品多关注战争对经济发展的影响。

25. **南森·纳恩**，加拿大学者，哈佛大学经济学教授，以其经济史研究特别是探讨经济与社会发展关系的著作而闻名。

26. **威廉·D. 帕蒂森**（1921—1997），美国地理学家，就职于芝加哥大学。其分析地理学科、探讨美国土地使用模式的学术专著在业界颇有影响力。

27. **法兰西斯克·皮泽洛**（1471—1541），西班牙殖民军队司令官。他指挥军队征服了印加帝国。1528 年，他成为该殖民地，即现秘鲁所在地的首位执政官。

28. **詹姆斯·罗宾逊**（1960 年生），英国经济学家、政治理论家，就职于哈佛大学。他在与德隆·阿西莫格鲁合著的《国家为什么会失败》一书中，强调了政策与体制在发展经济学中的作用。

29. **杰弗里·萨克斯**（1954 年生），美国经济学家，就职于哈佛大学。他的主要研究方向为可持续发展，特别是自然环境的可持续发展。他也帮助创立了联合国千年发展目标。

30. **林恩·斯皮尔曼**，美国圣母大学社会学教授。她的著作主要关注各种社会因素对政治战略的影响。

31. **朱利安·斯图尔德**（1902—1972），美国人类学家。主要研究人类如何操控环境以维持自身发展。

32. **保罗·斯特里坦**（1917—2019），英国奥地利裔美国发展经济学家。其著名的研究成果是，提出以"基本需求"法来研究经济发展，曾在 20 世纪 60 年代为英国海外发展部提供顾问咨询。

33. **斯图尔特·维斯**，康涅狄格学院心理学教授。主要研究领域是行为分析。

34. **伊曼纽尔·沃勒斯坦**（1930 年生），美国社会学家，世界体系理论代表人物。世界体系理论认为发达的"中心"国家（主要指西方国家）与边缘国家有不同的劳动分工。中心国家为获取利益而压榨边缘国家的资源和劳动力。

35. **安德鲁·沃纳**，美国经济学家，他致力于研究政府对本国发展投资方式与原因。

36. **斯蒂芬·韦特海姆**，美国青年历史学家。在哥伦比亚大学攻读硕士学位时，便在《国家》杂志发表了对戴蒙德著作的评论。

37. **迈克尔·威尔克斯**，美国斯坦福大学人类学副教授，主要研究美国西南部的土著历史。

38. **耶利**（1912—1975），巴布亚新几内亚政治家、社会活动家。他在自己的政治生涯中曾积极促进中央政府与各地组织之间的关系。

39. **诺曼·约菲**，纽约大学人类学和近东研究教授，主要研究古老的美索不达米亚文明以及古老国度兴衰背后的原因。

40. **理查德·约克**，俄勒冈大学社会学和环境研究教授，主要研究气候变化和人类对自然环境所产生的影响。

WAYS IN TO THE TEXT

KEY POINTS

- Jared Diamond's 1997 book *Guns, Germs, and Steel: The Fates of Human Societies* won the highly respected Pulitzer Prize* for General Nonfiction in 1998.

- In *Guns, Germs, and Steel*, Diamond argues that geographic factors have a significant influence on history.

- Diamond's book compares historical cases with very large spans of time and distance between them—that is, it uses the comparative method* of historical analysis on a very large scale.

Who Is Jared Diamond?

Jared Diamond, the author of *Guns, Germs, and Steel: The Fates of Human Societies*, was born in Boston in 1937. He is an American evolutionary biologist, anthropologist, ecologist, and historian. His father was a pediatrician—a doctor specializing in children—and his mother was a concert pianist and a teacher of languages; thanks, in part, to his mother's influence, he can speak 12 languages.

His interest in so many fields follows his training in biochemistry (the chemical processes that occur inside living things) at Harvard University in the US, and his later training in physiology (anatomical structures) in England, at Cambridge University. He finished his studies in 1965 and, after a stint at Harvard, became professor of physiology at the medical school of the University of California, Los Angeles (UCLA).At this point, his career as an ecologist was born.

He developed a passion for ornithology—the study of birds— and began visiting the South Pacific island of New Guinea regularly.

Although these trips were initially to study the island's birds, he also became attached to the people. A chance meeting with a local politician called Yali* sparked Diamond's interest in the development of human societies. In *Guns, Germs, and Steel*, Diamond applies his previous training to the analysis of human societies.

At the age of 65, Diamond completely abandoned his initial career in medical science and physiology, and devoted himself entirely to environmental history and evolutionary biology. He is now a professor of geography at UCLA, where he pursues his two other main interests: environmental activism that focuses on conservation efforts in New Guinea, and writing books about history aimed at general readers.

What Does *Guns, Germs, and Steel* Say?

Guns, Germs, and Steel is Jared Diamond's attempt to answer a question he was asked by Yali, the politician he met on one of his trips to New Guinea. "Why is it,"Yali asked, "that you white people developed so much cargo [that is, material goods] and brought it to New Guinea, but we black people had little cargo of our own?"[1] In effect, Yali wanted Diamond to give him an account of a phenomenon called "uneven development"*—the disparities in technology, wealth, standards of living, freedom, and other key factors, all around the world. Why, in short, are some countries "developed" and others "developing"?

Diamond's answer to this question focused on long-term causes; he examined, in fact, a 13,000-year span of history to argue that key moments that contributed to today's development imbalance took place between the fifteenth and nineteenth centuries, when Europeans conquered much of the world. But European conquest is only what Diamond calls the "proximate" cause (meaning the closest, most obvious factor driving the change). He is not interested in proximate causes, wanting to find the "ultimate" cause—the underlying, long-term factor—that gave rise to the proximate cause.

The answer, he finds, is to do with the invention of agriculture. When people give up hunting and gathering in favor of agriculture, he argues, they are no longer focused on subsistence—that is, meeting the needs of their immediate survival—by following resources such as seasonal rain and migrating animals. They are necessarily less mobile. And eventually, towns and cities are formed. Every member of a hunter-gatherer community* spends many hours looking for food. But in agricultural communities, only some work in food production; others work as leaders, scribes, warriors, smiths, scientists, and so on. And organization like this is required for the development of things such as writing and technology.

Diamond does not leave the argument there, however. Why is it, he asks, that some societies become agricultural in the first place? And to answer *that*, he points to geography. Plants and animals that can be easily domesticated* are unevenly distributed, he points out; the majority are in southwest and southeast Eurasia. And the arrangement of Eurasia itself along an east-west axis, as opposed to a north-south axis, makes the exchange of plants and ideas in this region easier.

Because Eurasia contains long stretches of similar land, societies throughout history have been able to share solutions to common problems. Beyond this region, however, where there were fewer plants and animals that could be domesticated, hunter-gatherers would not have been able to change their lifestyle even if the idea had occurred to them. Random geographical factors and the unequal distribution of resources, then, set the stage for modern international inequality.

When *Guns, Germs, and Steel* was published in 1997, it became an international phenomenon. It was awarded both the prestigious Pulitzer Prize in General Nonfiction and the Phi Beta Kappa Award in Science, awarded to significant books in science. It has been translated into 36 languages and is a fixture on undergraduate reading lists around the world. That is, in part, because of its application of the comparative method of historical analysis: it is an attempt to "do" history as a science.

Why Does *Guns, Germs, and Steel* Matter?

The book provides an introduction to the "comparative method" of history—the application of scientific reasoning to questions about historical causes. The comparative method aims to look at *similar* cases that produced *different* outcomes and *different* cases that produced *similar* outcomes. From this, important further questions arise: What was different in the two similar cases? What was similar in the different cases? This helps establish *causation*—that is, it explains which factor caused which outcome.

The comparative method is a powerful tool. It can be used

in nearly every discipline that looks at causes. For example, it is often used in the study of politics to establish conclusions. Students can look at countries that succeed in developing, and others that remain underdeveloped.* They can look at policy choices made in the past, and compare them to argue why they resulted in different outcomes.

Comparison and evidence are two key concepts in developing critical thinking. Critical thinking looks beyond surface-level ideas, and uses a rational system to understand what is really going on. A non-scientific approach to human history would have had little chance of identifying the causes of development 13,000 years ago.

Students can also develop critical thinking skills by looking at Diamond's critics. Even though Diamond is a critical historian who attempts to undermine the assumptions of others, he has some assumptions of his own. For example, some critics have suggested that Diamond's work is not as scientific as he says it is, and that he makes assumptions that are "culturally bound" (that is, he works with the assumption that certain Western ideas about what societies "should do" have a universal application).

---

1. Jared M. Diamond, *Guns, Germs, and Steel: The Fates of Human Societies* (New York: W. W. Norton & Company, 1999), 14.

SECTION 1
INFLUENCES

THE AUTHOR AND THE HISTORICAL CONTEXT

KEY POINTS

* *Guns, Germs, and Steel* presents a scientific study of inequality, using data from the past 13,000 years.

* Diamond's experience of life on the island of New Guinea inspired him to explore why some countries were underdeveloped* compared with others.

* The end of the Cold War* between the West and the former Soviet Union and the rise of globalization* (the interconnected nature of the world's economies, peoples, and cultures) put these questions at the forefront of debate.

Why Read This Text?

Jared Diamond's book *Guns, Germs, and Steel* examines the ultimate causes behind broad patterns of history. His argument is that, over the last 13,000 years of human history, contrasting paths of development between different peoples are the result of environmental differences between continents rather than biological differences between peoples. The title of the book refers to the proximate causes (that is, the immediate answers) to the question of why the European conquest of the Americas proceeded as it did. Diamond believes we cannot stop our inquiry there, however, and follows the chains of causation that show how each of these proximate factors result from an ultimate cause—environmental differences between continents and the rise of food production.

He attempts a scientific approach to human history, piecing together ideas from diverse disciplines to establish a broad theory about human development. He uses a comparative approach* borrowed from biology to test his theories relating to "broad patterns that occur across space and time that do not require environmental manipulation."[1] In other words, he compares historical circumstances divided by great geographical and chronological distances in order to discover why outcomes of different kinds occurred.

He conducts his search for answers by tracing the "chains of causation" beyond the factors that obviously affected the accumulation of power and wealth—guns, germs, and steel. According to his thesis, the ultimate causes that explain the different outcomes in human development are environmental differences between continents, and favorable or unfavorable conditions for the rise and spread of food production.

Guns, Germs, and Steel demonstrates that it is possible to take a broad and bold interdisciplinary approach to answering history's most important questions.

> "How big is the gap between rich and poor and what is happening to it? Very roughly and briefly: the difference in income per head between the richest industrial nation, say Switzerland, and the poorest non- industrial country, Mozambique, is about 400 to 1."
>
> —— David Landes, *The Wealth and Poverty of Nations*

Author's Life

Jared Diamond was born in Boston in 1937. His mother was a musician and amateur linguist, his father the associate chief of staff of the Children's Hospital at Harvard Medical School and a specialist in blood diseases. Diamond majored in biochemistry at Harvard College; throughout his schooling he expected to become a physician like his father. In the last undergraduate year, however, he shifted his focus to biological research and studied as a postgraduate at Cambridge University in England for a PhD in physiology.

World War II* was an important factor in shaping Diamond's world-view. He traveled through Europe after his PhD and learned how people's experiences of the war had shaped their lives."Depending on whether they are English, German, Finnish, or Yugoslav," Diamond said, "born in 1937, I immediately knew whether their lives had suffered some major disruption" such as losing parents or homes. His conclusion was that "it was just an accident of whether they had been born in London, Berlin, Helsinki, or Zagreb."[2] This concern with the ways in which our opportunities are shaped by our circumstances would come to the fore later in his career.

His focus shifted away from medical laboratory research in 1964 when he traveled to the Pacific island of New Guinea, where he developed a passion for ecology and biology. As he became increasingly interested in the wildlife and people of New Guinea, his career also changed. His earlier focus on medicine and anatomy expanded to history, geography, ecology, biology, and anthropology. Although Diamond never had any formal training in these fields, he has published many papers since the 1970s, influenced by his 26 trips to New Guinea for field research.

Author's Background

Diamond wrote *Guns, Germs, and Steel* in the mid-1990s. For much of his life—from 1945 to 1989—world politics had been shaped by the Cold War and the antagonistic relationship between the United States and the Soviet Union.

In the aftermath of the Cold War, though, new relationships— between developed and developing countries,and between developing countries themselves—took on a new importance."We live in stirring times," opens the United Nations'* 1990 *Human Development Report*; political systems and economic structures, it continues,"are beginning to change in countries where democratic forces had long been suppressed."[3] In other words, connections between the developed and the developing world were increasing in number and importance—and questions arose as to why some nations remained undeveloped, and what could be done about it.

The American economist and historian David Landes,* whose book *The Wealth and Poverty of Nations* was published at about the same time as Diamond's, suggests why it was timely and important to account for this uneven development.* "The old division of the world into two power blocs, East and West, has subsided," he wrote, and in the aftermath of ideological stand-offs and looming nuclear war "the big challenge and threat is the gap in wealth and health that separates rich and poor."[4] If the problems of development and uneven development are to be addressed, then their ultimate causes need to be discovered. Both Diamond and Landes aimed to uncover the root causes.

---

1. Christopher Miller, "Review of *Guns, Germs, and Steel: The Fate of Human Societies*, by Jared M. Diamond," *Economic Botany* 56, no. 2 (2002): 209.

2. Jared Diamond, "About Me," accessed May 30, 2015, http://www. jareddiamond.org/Jared_Diamond/About_Me.html.

3. Mahbub ul-Haq, ed., *Human Development Report 1990* (New York: Oxford University Press, 1990), iii.

4. David Landes, *The Wealth and Poverty of Nations: Why Some Are So Rich and Some Are So Poor* (New York: W. W. Norton & Company, 1998), xx.

MODULE 2
ACADEMIC CONTEXT

KEY POINTS

* The study of "man-land"* geography emphasizes the relationship between humanity and its environment.

* In the work of such scientists as the influential English naturalist Charles Darwin* (who famously described the principles of evolution in 1859) and the French historian Fernand Braudel* (who founded the Annales school* of history), the scientific method has been used to explain the relationship between underlying factors and results.

* The scientific method crosses over to other, related, social science disciplines such as processual archaeology* (which seeks to establish "laws" of human behavior to explain archaeological evidence) and environmental sociology (which seeks to understand social behavior in the context of the environment).

The Work in Its Context

Jared Diamond's *Guns, Germs, and Steel* is an interdisciplinary work—it draws on the aims and methods of different academic disciplines. Although it is relevant to the study of history, politics, and physical sciences, it is particularly relevant to the study of geography.

According to the American geographer William D. Pattison,* there are four main traditions of geography: the spatial tradition, the area studies tradition, the earth science tradition, and the "man-land" tradition.[1] "Spatial" geography compares the "distance, form, direction, and position" of different things and focuses mainly on maps and the physical features of the land."Area studies" is interested in "the nature of places, their character and their differentiation" beyond their physical features; it usually focuses on describing socio-political differences, rather than analyzing their origins."Earth science," such as the study of geology, applies physics and chemistry to understanding the physical world.[2] Of these, Diamond's book is in the "man-land" tradition.

"Man-land" approaches to geography, which often include aspects of sociology (the study of the history and functioning of human society), look at the interaction between places (geography) and people (sociology), and how this shapes events throughout time (history). Structuralism,* an approach to the study of human culture founded on the idea that human actions are shaped by their place in a larger system,[3] is particularly important to man-land studies. In Diamond's case, the important factors of the larger system are environmental.

> "New [processual] archaeology stressed theory formation, model building, and hypothesis testing in the search for general laws of human behavior. Perhaps its most important contribution was its focus on culture process rather than culture history."
> ——Timothy K. Earle and Robert W. Preucel, "Processual Archaeology and the Radical Critique"

Overview of the Field

In his deeply influential book *On the Origin of Species* (1859), the

English naturalist Charles Darwin examines the relationship between creatures and plants and their environments. His theory of natural selection* showed how environmental conditions shaped particular characteristics through "the preservation of favorable variations and the rejection of injurious variations."[4] This idea is relevant to our topic in its understanding of the role of nature. Darwin's idea that, over time, nature makes "winners" and "losers" was applied (or, rather, *misapplied*) to account for variations among human societies.

The American geographer Ellsworth Huntington's* book *Civilization and Climate* (1915) is an example of such a misapplication. In it, he argues that there is a relationship between climate and society. "We realize that a dense and progressive population cannot live in the far North or in deserts simply because the difficulty of getting a living grinds men down and keeps them isolated."[5] Huntington's insight is to connect a particular culture to the needs of living in a certain place. His argument becomes problematic, however, when he emphasizes the role of race, comparing "Teutons" (German speakers) and "negroes" (people of African descent). Huntington believes that "as the plum differs from the apple not only in outward form and color, but in inward flavor, so the negro seems to differ from the white man ... in the workings of the mind."[6] This idea—that non-white people are naturally inferior and that their civilizations are destined to be inferior—was used for centuries to justify the expansion of European empires.

The French historian Fernand Braudel and the Annales school with which he was associated, named after the journal of historical inquiry that he co-edited, took a much broader view. This approach examines the *longue durée**—the long-term and invisible factors that shape events and whose change is so slow as to be invisible (the slow depletion of a forest, for example, that changes the nature of a local economy, and that in turn could give rise to a new government).

For Braudel, the "general conditions of human life" are not the edicts of kings, but the earth's peninsulas, seas, and mountains; non-human factors, in other words, shape human outcomes. Braudel's seminal book, *The Mediterranean World in the Age of Philip II* (1949), begins with an analysis of the *physical* environment of the Mediterranean world in the 1500s.Although Braudel's period of focus in the book is short—1550 to 1600—the matter of his study comes from "evidence, images, and landscapes dating from other periods ... [combined] across time and space."[7]

Academic Influences

Diamond was deeply influenced by the idea that the physical environment created the structures from which outcomes emerged. In his book, he applies it to archaeology. The American anthropologist Julien Steward,* who subscribes to the school of processual archaeology and its scientific rather than historical approach to the field of archaeology, writes that "All men eat, but this is an organic and not a cultural fact ... What and how different groups of men eat is a cultural fact explainable only by culture history and environmental factors."[8]

Processual archaeology is not only interested in "organic" facts but "cultural facts." An organic fact might be evidence that people ate wheat; a "cultural fact" might be what it *meant* to them, and what we can learn from that about ancient agriculture in general.This approach sees archaeology not as a window into a static moment in time but as a series of clues from which we can both deduce facts about ancient peoples and draw conclusions about human behavior in general.

As well as processual archaeology, Diamond was influenced by the field of environmental sociology. Developed by the American sociologists Riley Dunlap* and William Catton,* it "involves recognition of the fact that physical environments can influence (and in turn be influenced by) human societies and behavior."[9] This was a new turn in sociology, which until this point had been interested, for the most part, in the ways in which groups of people relate to one another. Introducing the environment as a new variable brought "man-land" geography and sociology together.

1. William D. Pattison, "The Four Traditions of Geography," *Journal of Geography* 63, no. 5 (1964): 211–16.

2. Pattison, "The Four Traditions of Geography," 211–16.

3. Pattison, "The Four Traditions of Geography."

4. Charles Darwin, *On the Origin of Species* (Oxford: Oxford University Press, 2008), 64.

5. Ellsworth Huntington, *Civilization and Climate* (New Haven, CT: Yale University Press, 1915), 2.

6. Huntington, *Civilization and Climate*, 16.

7. Fernand Braudel, *The Mediterranean World in the Age of Philip II: Volume I* (London: University of California Press, 1995), 23.

8. Julien Steward, *Theory of Culture Change: The Methodology of Multilinear Evolution* (Chicago: University of Illinois Press, 1972), 8.

9. Riley Dunlap and William Catton, "Environmental Sociology," *Annual Review of Sociology* 5 (1979): 244.

MODULE 3
THE PROBLEM

KEY POINTS

* Academics asked why there was inequality between states, given that people are the same around the world (no group of people is inherently cleverer or more inventive).

* World-systems theory* attributed underdevelopment* to oppression; many other theories of uneven development* argued it was due to divergences between Europe and the rest of the world in the seventeenth century.

* Diamond looked much further into the past. He argued that the explanations centered on the seventeenth century were not explaining the real causes, which were to be found in prehistory.

Core Question

As we have seen, Jared Diamond frames the core question of *Guns, Germs, and Steel* in terms of a question put to him by a New Guinean named Yali,* a friend of Diamond's and a local politician."Why is it," he asked, "that you white people developed so much cargo [material goods] and brought it to New Guinea, but we black people had little cargo of our own?"[1] Yali was asking why some parts of the world experienced rapid economic development and other parts did not, a question that became extremely important in the latter half of the twentieth century as the process of globalization*—the process by which the world becomes more closely integrated culturally, economically, and politically— became increasingly prevalent.

Given the close and increasing contact between cultures with different levels of economic development, it was increasingly important to account for these differences. Diamond, a scientist to the core, was determined not to frame this question in terms of simple and somewhat offensive causes related to technology, intelligence, and culture. Instead he tried a more rigorous methodological approach. For this reason, Diamond's question is not "Why is there inequality?" but rather "What is the real source of all the factors that have led to inequality?" Posing this question led Diamond's investigation back in time 13,000 years.

> "Oriental civilizations struck Europeans as monumental and grand. Much of the apparent grandeur was a compound of imposing works of civil engineering and luxury for the court circles. Mechanical engineering lagged.The standard of living of the mass of the people languished ... Overall, these societies were not rich in the sense of high average real incomes, the dimension in which Europe was to surpass them."
>
> —— Eric Jones, *The European Miracle*

The Participants

Other thinkers approaching this question tended to place the moment of divergence that resulted in European dominance in the sixteenth and seventeenth centuries.

Immanuel Wallerstein's* "world systems theory" was one of the key explanations of different levels of development.The theory rested on the differences between "core" and "periphery" nations in terms of who performed the labor required for certain nations to prosper. "In the late fifteenth and early sixteenth century," Wallerstein argued, "there came into existence what we may call a European world-economy."[2] By this, he means that labor came to be divided between European core nations and non-European periphery nations. "In the geo-economically peripheral areas of the emerging world-economy," he continued, "there were two principal activities: mines [and] agriculture." Resources from these mines and plantations were forcibly transported back to the core nations.[3]

Wallerstein locates the origins of this situation in the capitalist* ideology of Western Europe, according to which those who perform labor do their work with resources and tools owned by those who profit. So capitalism requires the existence of owning classes and working classes.

The British Australian economic historian Eric Jones's* seminal book *The European Miracle*, written in 1981, argues (in line with the earlier arguments of Fernand Braudel* and Wallerstein) that the moment in which it was decided that Europe would dominate the world occurred in the sixteenth century, when the continent "underwent those political, technological, and geographical upheavals which were to make it the birthplace of the industrial world."[4] These upheavals arose from a multitude of factors, from Europe's geography to its style of political organization.

Europe's rapid advances in technology from the sixteenth century onward were unique because, as Jones argued, "cultural connections and the competitive nature of the states system encouraged continual borrowing and 'stimulus diffusion' which meant that if a problem were solved in one country it was assumed it could be solved in another."⁵ In other words, European countries were separate enough to compete but close enough for solutions to common problems to spread rapidly. This analysis of the conjunctions of people and place is typical of Jones's approach.

The Contemporary Debate

In *Guns, Germs, and Steel*, Diamond writes that he sets his own argument against those based, like Ellsworth Huntington's,* on racial pseudo-science—non-scientific arguments that adopt the language of science."Probably the commonest explanation" for the different levels of development between Europe and the rest of the world, he writes, "involves implicitly or explicitly assuming biological differences among peoples."⁶ Diamond does not necessarily argue against academic arguments that involve this implicit prejudice; indeed such arguments became discredited generations ago. He argues, rather, against broad cultural assumptions outside academia.

His book is a far more popular work than others written in the second half of the twentieth century. Unlike most academic works, it is written mostly in non-academic language and without citation. In fact, one of the criticisms of Diamond's book was that it failed almost entirely to take part in the debates of the time in geography, history, or archaeology.⁷

Who, then, is Diamond really challenging? He is confronting those arguments that trace inequality to a "moment" of divergence in the fifteenth and sixteenth centuries, when Europe leapt ahead in its population, food production, and technology. This, though, only answers part of the question. Diamond believes nobody has looked adequately at the underlying cause of divergence—nor the underlying causes of those underlying causes.

---

1. Jared M. Diamond, *Guns, Germs, and Steel: The Fates of Human Societies* (New York: W. W. Norton & Company, 1999), 14.
2. Immanuel Wallerstein, *The Modern World System I: Capitalist Agriculture and the Origins of the European World Economy in the Sixteenth Century* (London: University of California Press, 2011), 15.
3. Wallerstein, *The Modern World System*, 100.
4. Eric Jones, *The European Miracle: Environments, Economies, and Geopolitics in the History of Europe and Asia* (Cambridge: Cambridge University Press 2003), 225.
5. Jones, *The European Miracle*, 45.
6. Diamond, *Guns, Germs, and Steel*, 18–19.
7. Richard York and Philip Mancus, "Diamond in the Rough: Reflections on *Guns, Germs, and Steel*," *Research in Human Ecology* 14, no. 2 (2007): 159.

MODULE 4
THE AUTHOR'S CONTRIBUTION

KEY POINTS

* Diamond believes the roots of modern inequality are to be found in geography, which is the only thing that differentiated societies 13,000 years ago (before the invention of agriculture).

* Diamond's approach combined many different fields— geology, archaeology, sociology, and others—using natural experiments* (that is, the opportunity to compare groups of people living in different conditions to understand why they arrived at different outcomes).

* Diamond broadened the scale and scope of a question about human development that had been asked throughout the twentieth century.

Author's Aims

Jared Diamond summarized his key argument in *Guns, Germs, and Steel* in one sentence:"History followed different courses for different people because of differences among peoples' environments, not because of biological differences among peoples themselves."[1]

The main focus of Diamond's book, however, is not merely the rejection of "biological" theories of difference. He wants, rather, to search beyond explanations that provide "parts of the puzzle, but ... provide only pieces of the needed broad synthesis that has been missing."[2] This is a "structural"* exploration of history—it focuses on the ways in which human behavior outcomes are shaped by factors outside people's control.

Diamond intended his work to explore "ultimate" rather

than "proximate" causes of Western dominance—that is, the foundational causes, not the immediate causes. To do this, he had to trace the fundamental factors that enabled this dominance. Diamond believed that if an analysis should find that Western dominance occurred due to technological superiority, then that analysis was not thorough enough. If being ahead in technology allowed the West to dominate, then what was the reason for this technological superiority? This question cannot be answered without an analysis that considers some 13,000 years of history and accounts for the beginnings of civilization—far earlier than the fifteenth century, when consequences with ancient origins were felt in the colonized world.

> *"A technique that frequently proves fruitful in ... historical disciplines is the so-called natural experiment or the comparative method. This approach consists of comparing ... different systems that are similar in many respects but differ with respect to the factors whose influence one wishes to study."*
>
> ——Jared Diamond and James Robinson, *Natural Experiments of History*

Approach

Jared Diamond takes a scientific approach to the study of history in *Guns, Germs, and Steel*, and uses archaeological and environmental evidence from the physical world to build his argument. His book begins with an examination of "human history on all the continents, for millions of years, from our origins as a species until 13,000 years ago";[3] his aim is to present "human history as a science, on a par with acknowledged historical sciences such as astronomy, geology, and evolutionary biology."[4]

Since Diamond does not have a laboratory where he can run controlled experiments on different populations, he takes advantage of what he calls "natural experiments" by comparing two populations that differ in a certain way—a population that develops agriculture and another that does not, for example.[5] As a result, some of Diamond's comparisons are drawn on a large scale. They look at continent-sized regions that differ in their plant and animal populations, or their climate, or other factors. He uses these factors to draw conclusions about why some societies became centralized, complex, and technologically sophisticated while others did not. He looks at archaeological evidence such as the remains of plants and animals to identify which crops were domesticated,* where, and at what times.

His argument always proceeds from physical evidence (characteristics such as natural docility or rapid growth rate) to social conclusions (cultures that could domesticate animals had access to more advantages), and he bases his argument on comparisons.

Contribution in Context

Diamond was not the first man-land* geographer—that is, a geographer whose analysis considers the environmental context of historical events—to look at the broad distinctions that have set human societies on their different paths, nor the first to look for ultimate causes in the deep recesses of prehistory.

In his 1972 book *The Colombian Exchange*, the American historian Alfred Crosby* reflected on the process of intercontinental exchange between the Old World (Asia, Africa, and Europe) and the New (the Americas, Australia). Crosby's account of the meeting of the Old and New Worlds has similarities to Diamond's. "When Columbus* arrived, even the most advanced [Native Americans] were barely out of the Stone Age,* and their armies were swept aside by tiny bands of conquistadors."* Furthermore, they had "few domesticated animals," and "died in droves of diseases" that had become commonplace in the Old World.⁶

The focus of Crosby's argument, however, is only partly on how Europeans came to dominate the world. Much of his book is dedicated to tracking the consequences of the sudden bringing together of two landmasses separated for millennia; many of these consequences were biological: some species became extinct while others spread around the world. In other words, Crosby is interested in the ways in which the powerful Europeans brought their crops and animals across the sea, and brought back others from the Americas.

Diamond is more interested in the original conditions that allowed the Europeans to be in this position. So although his work may share Crosby's focus in many ways, his contribution lies in the scale and scope of the proof of his theory.

1. Jared M. Diamond, *Guns, Germs, and Steel: The Fates of Human Societies* (New York: W. W. Norton & Company, 1999), 25.

2. Diamond, *Guns, Germs, and Steel*, 24.

3. Diamond, *Guns, Germs, and Steel*, 37.

4. Diamond, *Guns, Germs, and Steel*, 408.

5. Diamond, *Guns, Germs, and Steel*, 424.

6. Alfred W. Crosby, *The Colombian Exchange: Biological and Cultural Consequences of 1492* (Westport, CT: Praeger, 2003), 21.

SECTION 2
IDEAS

MAIN IDEAS

KEY POINTS

- The key themes of *Guns, Germs, and Steel* are the distribution of natural goods and features throughout the world; the role of those resources in encouraging agriculture; and the role of agriculture in encouraging development.

- Eurasia had the right mix of crops, animals, and geographical features to encourage settlement in cities, and therefore complexity (guns and steel) and robust immune systems (germs); the rest of the world did not.

- Diamond wrote this book for a popular, rather than an academic, audience, and it led to some criticism that the book is not rigorous enough.

Key Themes

The key themes of Jared Diamond's *Guns, Germs, and Steel* concern some of the most basic building blocks of civilization. The core argument concerns the naturally unequal distribution of crops such as wheat that are easy to cultivate and animals such as the goat that are easy to domesticate.* This unevenness meant that people living in different regions experienced different developmental paths.

Diamond's overall question is: what are the *ultimate* causes of inequality between regions of the world? The themes he explores are natural—crops, animals, and terrain. In Eurasia, these factors gave rise to both social complexity and disease, and thereby set the stage for these societies, and particularly those of Western Europe, to dominate the rest of the world.

Understanding Diamond's aim in *Guns, Germs, and Steel* means understanding, too, the difference between "proximate" causes—an apple falls from a tree because it is shaken by a stiff breeze, for example—and "ultimate" causes—the causes that might explain why *that* apple fell when other apples on nearby trees did not. The "ultimate" cause may be that the tree that shed apples was on a poor patch of land without much nutrition, and the stems attaching the apples to the tree were weaker. Both answers are right. But one is more comprehensive.

> *"When Pizarro* and Atahuallpa* met at Cajamarca,* why did Pizarro capture Atahuallpa and kill so many of his followers, instead of Atahuallpa's vastly more numerous forces capturing and killing Pizarro? After all, Pizarro had only 62 soldiers mounted on horses, along with 106 foot soldiers, while Atahuallpa commanded an army of about 80,000."*
>
> ——Jared Diamond, *Guns, Germs, and Steel*

Exploring the Ideas

Diamond's overall argument is that today's profoundly unequal world is the result of geographic inequalities in the natural world, rather than genetic inequalities such as some peoples having higher intelligence than others. These geographic inequalities include both crops and animals that lend themselves to domestication (the process by which wild animals and plants are "tamed" by selective breeding for features that serve human beings) and features of the terrain.

Europeans, for instance, became advanced at warfare because their continent is naturally broken up by mountains and rivers into small societies that were prone to conflict. Rather than hunting and gathering naturally occurring food, the fertile land and access to fresh water in Europe allowed for "food production," which "was indirectly a prerequisite for the development of guns, germs, and steel."[1]

Food production was not, Diamond argues, "invented" by some clever people around the world who had a better idea than hunting and gathering—rather it "evolved" slowly.[2] Several factors underlie the origins of food production. The availability of crops that are easily domesticated is one. Oats, for instance, require little in the way of selective breeding to make them easily farmed, whereas corn requires a great deal. Crops were domesticated to yield larger amounts of food. Similarly, dogs were domesticated to be docile and friendly to their masters.

Eurasia started off with many easily domesticated staple crops—wheat, barley, lentils, and so forth—whereas the Americas did not. Moreover, a complete package is necessary to make the switch worthwhile. This means there must be enough high-yielding cereal crops, large land animals to work the fields (and eventually become a food source themselves), and a temperate climate.* "The reason," Diamond argues, "Native Americans did not domesticate apples lay with the entire suite of wild plant and animal species available to Native Americans";

there was only modest potential for domestication available to them.[3] Domesticating plants and animals involves a fundamental change in ways of life—so for any to occur at all, it must be very worthwhile.

How does food production give rise to guns, germs, and steel? Food production supports dense populations, which in turn "led to the proximate causes of germs, literacy, technology, and centralized government." And this led to Eurasian world domination.[4] When humans live close to animals, and close to one another in cities, diseases can readily make the jump across species and quickly become commonplace among entire populations (smallpox, for instance, originated in cattle).[5] Density, however, begets technology as well as germs."A stored food surplus" in an agricultural society "can support... full time specialists," from kings and bureaucrats to blacksmiths, scholars, and soldiers.[6] Conversely, in communities that live by hunting and gathering, everyone is required to spend many hours in finding and processing food. So the scribes and blacksmiths of agricultural societies have the time to develop new inventions—writing systems, tools, and weapons—that pave the way for yet more advanced inventions.

Diamond calls this an "autocatalytic" process, which simply means that it is a process that builds on itself: bronze working allows humans to use more advanced tools to mine iron, which allows them to make yet more advanced tools. Therefore, we come to see how food production "makes complex societies possible."[7] Eurasia was naturally, and arbitrarily, endowed with the geographical features that give rise to food production. This in turn gave rise to technology, which enabled more advanced technology and the exchanges of ideas with other complex societies—which gave rise to further advancement.

Language and Expression

Guns, Germs, and Steel was written for a mass audience—most reviewers praised "its erudition, clear prose, and elegant synthesis of multiple sources, from archaeology to zoology."[8] Diamond uses colorful examples generously, explains academic concepts throughout, and does not use overlong or complicated sentences. Moreover, he uses graphs throughout the book to illustrate complex concepts—especially worthwhile is the graphical summary of his entire model of ultimate causes of history, compressed into a single page.[9]

Although the book is highly readable and engaging, it has been criticized for its lack of academic referencing. While Diamond presents a "further reading list" at the end of the work, there are few, if any, citations in the text. Some reviewers have criticized *Guns, Germs, and Steel* for getting its facts wrong, and focusing on making an elegant argument that would appeal to a mass audience (and the judges of literary prizes), rather than an academically rigorous one.[10]

Students reading *Guns, Germs, and Steel* should keep in mind that Diamond is balancing commercial appeal and academic rigor.

1. Jared M. Diamond, *Guns, Germs, and Steel: The Fates of Human Societies* (New York: W. W. Norton & Company, 1999), 86.

2. Diamond, *Guns, Germs, and Steel*, 104.

3. Diamond, *Guns, Germs, and Steel*, 156.

4. Diamond, *Guns, Germs, and Steel*, 195.

5. Diamond, *Guns, Germs, and Steel*, 207.

6. Diamond, *Guns, Germs, and Steel*, 90.

7. Diamond, *Guns, Germs, and Steel*, 286.

8. Robin McKie, "Jared Diamond: What We Can Learn from Tribal Life," *Guardian*, January 6, 2013, accessed July 17, 2015, http://www. theguardian.com/science/2013/jan/06/jared-diamond-tribal-life-anthropology.

9. Diamond, *Guns, Germs, and Steel*, 87.

10. Andrew Sluyter, "Neo-Environmental Determinism, Intellectual Damage Control, and Nature/ Society Science," *Antipode* 35, no. 4 (2003): 813.

MODULE 6
SECONDARY IDEAS

KEY POINTS

* Eurasia was destined to dominate because of its basket of natural goods; Europe was destined to dominate within this system because of its terrain features.

* China is too geographically and politically unified to develop dependably; bad decisions made by emperors tend not to get reversed.

* Although Diamond's book is remembered more for its content than its methodology, recent scholarship has become interested in exploring natural experiments.*

Other Ideas

Jared Diamond's key themes in *Guns, Germs, and Steel* concern the global history of development based on environmental factors. His secondary ideas relate to how particular areas of the Old World developed differently—he focuses in particular on China and Africa. The Old World, after all, was geographically linked—and food production arose indigenously in Africa and China.

There is another key factor here, however: the advantages of an East-West orientation. "As one moves along a north-south axis," he writes, "one traverses zones differing greatly" in terms of climate, native species of plants and animals, and terrain. This made it hard to share both domesticated* plants and animals and technology; along an East-West axis where the climate remains broadly consistent, however, it is much simpler.[1]

This observation leads Diamond to another interesting question. Both Europe and China sat along the East-West axis of Eurasia, and both enjoyed indigenous food production and rapid technological advance. So what explains historical European dominance? To answer the question, Diamond turns to the way that geography affects politics in complex societies.

> *"A larger area or population means more potential inventors, more competing societies, more innovations available to adopt—and more pressure to adopt and retain innovations, because societies failing to do so will tend to be eliminated by competing societies."*
>
> ——Jared Diamond, *Guns, Germs, and Steel*

Exploring the Ideas

"Until around a.d.1450,"Diamond argues,"China was technologically much more innovative and advanced than Europe [but] then ceased to be innovative."[2] Diamond lays out a number of proximate causes rooted in European society: the development of a merchant class and the economic system of capitalism;* patent protection for inventions; its comparative lack of political regimes founded on absolute despotism* (that is, where power was concentrated in very few hands) and crushing taxation; and its Greco-Judeo-Christian tradition of empirical* inquiry"[3] (that is, the scientific tradition of basing conclusions on observable evidence).

Again, the ultimate causes behind these proximate causes, Diamond finds, are geographical—and political unity is key to this problem. China, as a society, was too unified. This meant that temporary "backward" or poor decisions become permanent; Diamond cites a political dispute in the Chinese court leading to the permanent dismantling of its ocean-going fleet in the fifteenth century.[4] Europe, on the other hand, was politically fragmented— so, if one society made a backward decision, it was likely another would learn from it. Diamond gives the example of the Italian explorer Christopher Columbus,* who "succeeded on his fifth try in persuading one of Europe's hundreds of princes to sponsor" his voyage across the Atlantic.[5]

In other words, China's structure meant mistakes made by rulers would be implemented across the entire country, whereas Europe's structure meant that while several princes might not see the value of the voyage, eventually one would. Then, as others became aware of the success of the first voyage, "best practice" would ensure they would naturally want to follow in those footsteps.

What is the geographic basis of Europe's fragmentation? It is a continent divided by rivers, peninsulas, islands, and mountains, and so "Europe has many scattered small core areas, none big enough to dominate the others for long, and each the center of chronically independent states."[6] China, on the other hand, has fewer and comparatively small islands, and was unified by 221 B.C.E. Its divided nature meant Europe only began the process of unification in the twentieth century—and even now, it is a far from assured process.[7] Diamond argues that China's connectedness was an advantage at first, as it could devote vast resources to developing a complex, advanced society. However, Europe's structure meant that "if one state did not pursue some particular innovation, another did, forcing neighboring states to do likewise" or face domination, economically or militarily.[8]

Overlooked

Guns, Germs, and Steel is a notably cohesive work in terms of its argument and structure. In the light of this, it is its methodology of "history-as-science" rather than its content that has been somewhat overlooked.

The American psychologist Stuart Vyse* thinks Diamond's scientific approach to understanding social outcomes has benefits for other disciplines. Behavior analysis, he says,"could be introduced into new areas of public dialogue if more behavior analysts followed Diamond's lead and conducted scientific histories."[9] Vyse suggests that social problems with behavioral rather than genetic origins "such as aggression, crime, and alcohol and drug addiction" may be affected by important environmental factors that are "yet to be articulated."[10] Diamond's method using grand comparisons is, for Vyse, a way to obtain real knowledge about social realities without the need for laboratory conditions.* While the tradition of "natural experiments" in social analysis has a long history, and is well rooted in policy analysis today, Diamond has done much, Vyse says, to prove that it can be applied on yet grander scales.

One example of such an application was a natural experiment by David Humphreys* and colleagues at the University of Oxford.

They used existing data to evaluate a new rule about the sale of alcohol in the British city of Manchester to investigate whether the removal of regulations on the time of day alcohol is sold would lead to an increase in anti-social behavior. Police incident reports before and after the rule change provided a means to measure the change.Their conclusion was that an increase in incidents late at night occurred after the rule change (but not an increase overall). This is not a controlled experiment, but a "natural" experiment, making use of the wider world to draw conclusions about the proximate and ultimate causes of social outcomes.[11]

1. Jared M. Diamond, *Guns, Germs, and Steel: The Fates of Human Societies* (New York: W. W. Norton & Company, 1999), 399.

2. Diamond, *Guns, Germs, and Steel*, 253.

3. Diamond, *Guns, Germs, and Steel*, 410.

4. Diamond, *Guns, Germs, and Steel*, 412.

5. Diamond, *Guns, Germs, and Steel*, 413.

6. Diamond, *Guns, Germs, and Steel*, 414.

7. Diamond, *Guns, Germs, and Steel*, 414.

8. Diamond, *Guns, Germs, and Steel*, 416.

9. Stuart Vyse, "World History for Behavior Analysts: Jared Diamond's *Guns, Germs, and Steel*," *Behavior and Social Issues* 11, no. 1 (2001): 85.

10. Vyse, "World History for Behavior Analysts," 86.

11. David K. Humphreys et al., "Evaluating the Impact of Flexible Alcohol Trading Hours on Violence: An Interrupted Time Series Analysis," *PLOS ONE* 8, no. 2 (2013): 1, accessed July 15, 2015, doi:10.1371/journal.pone.0055581.

MODULE 7
ACHIEVEMENT

KEY POINTS

* Diamond's theory in *Guns, Germs, and Steel* is one of the most rigorous theories of world history.

* Some critics argue that this is not a real theory, but a backward-looking justification of existing distributions of power.

* Critics argue that some groups Diamond claims were eradicated by Europeans actually still exist.

Assessing the Argument

Is the "grand" theory of Jared Diamond's *Guns, Germs, and Steel* convincing? The answer is both "yes" and "no." It is possible that Diamond does not actually derive any laws at all—he merely explains what has already happened. So, the Old World conquers the New, and Europe emerges victorious as though it could only have happened this way. This question—whether or not history, as a discipline, lends itself to parsimonious* explanations—is asked by the right-wing economist Gene Callahan* of the Ludwig von Mises Institute,*1 an organization that argues for less government interference in the free market.

"Parsimony" in this context means that a complex set of outcomes can be explained with reference to one critically important factor—in this case, Diamond explains all of human history with reference to the distribution of a very few factors. Callahan suggests that parsimonious explanations are possible in the natural sciences—an apple, released from a height, will always

113

fall—"but no similar facts are given to the historian."[2]

Whether or not laws actually govern history and other social sciences is still up for debate.Assuming that it *is* possible for history to be governed by laws, then Diamond's argument is successful. This would also assume that because things happened in a certain way, they could not have happened any other way over the long term. But if by "history" we mean a succession of singular events affecting one another in unpredictable ways, then the grand theory of *Guns, Germs, and Steel* is not successful.

> " While Diamond's book is filled with valuable insights, it is not, as he would like to believe, the first step in the reformation of history along more 'scientific' lines, but only another interesting vantage point from which to contemplate humanity's past. Furthermore, the policy implications of his overreach are a danger to both human welfare and freedom."
> ——Gene Callahan, "The Diamond Fallacy"

Achievement in Context

Diamond's *Guns, Germs, and Steel* was an enormously successful book. It won the prestigious Pulitzer Prize* for General Nonfiction in 1998, and has been translated into 36 languages. In the United States, the National Geographic Society produced a TV series based on the book which was broadcast in 2005. What is more telling, though, is that it won the Phi Beta Kappa Award in Science in 1997—an award given to works of science literature, which lends support to Diamond's claim that history (and geography) can genuinely be a science.

In their review of the book, "Diamond in the Rough," the American sociologists Richard York* and Philip Mancus* speculate why it was that *Guns, Germs, and Steel* had such commercial success but relatively little direct impact on the discipline of environmental sociology,* especially given its high level of scientific rigor. "This is ironic," they say, "since environmental sociology ... is fundamentally concerned with how human societies are both affected by and affect their environments."[3]

Diamond's parsimonious scientific perspective was one reason for this lack of impact. It was in stark contrast to another phenomenon in the social sciences often called the "cultural turn," which came into prominence in the early 1990s.The cultural turn—described as "one of the most influential trends in the humanities and social sciences in the last generation" by the American sociologists Mark Jacobs* and Lyn Spillman*—sees social science as a tool for exploring meanings in specific contexts, rather than deriving universal laws.[4] In effect, Diamond's ideas were out of step with current trends. As a result, Diamond's work went on to be more influential in development economics than sociology.

Limitations

The American anthropologist Michael Wilcox* argues that many people would find *Guns, Germs, and Steel* (and *Collapse*, a later book) ridiculous. His reasoning is that Diamond ignores the perspectives of people he claims were completely eradicated, such as Native Americans, even though they continue to exist today, albeit in a different way. He argues that the idea that Native American societies have "collapsed" is actually a popular myth—"the popular narratives of conquest and disappearance are just that—a mythology."[5] He asks, "What if archaeologists were asked to explain the continued presence of descendant communities five hundred years after Columbus,* instead of their disappearance or marginality?"[6]

Wilcox argues that Diamond's "terminal narratives"—the idea that native communities reached an "end" when colonization* occurred—are not just questionable in their accuracy, but incredibly damaging to the psyche of the remaining native communities. In the "terminal" narrative,"abandoned sites" of native cities are interpreted as evidence of social collapse. Wilcox counters that "[the] other interpretation is one that envisions archaeological sites the way Native peoples see them: as part of a living cosmological and historical landscape," still inhabited by native peoples.[7]

The core of Wilcox's discussion of the limitations of *Guns, Germs, and Steel* is perspective: Diamond assumes that native culture collapsed, and is now an artifact of the past, but this denies the existence of still-living Native Americans. Clearly, Native Americans would reject his thesis.

---

1. Gene Callahan, "The Diamond Fallacy," Mises Institute, accessed May 17, 2015, https://mises.org/library/diamond-fallacy.

2. Callahan, "The Diamond Fallacy."

3. Richard York and Philip Mancus, "Diamond in the Rough: Reflections on *Guns, Germs, and Steel*,"

Research in Human Ecology 14, no. 2 (2007): 157.

4. Mark D. Jacobs and Lyn Spillman, "Cultural Sociology at the Crossroads of a Discipline," *Poetics* 33 (2005): 1.

5. Michael Wilcox, "Marketing Conquest and the Vanishing Indian: An Indigenous Response to Jared Diamond's *Guns, Germs, and Steel,*" *Journal of Social Archaeology* 10, no. 1 (2010): 96.

6. Michael Wilcox, *The Pueblo Revolt and the Mythology of Conquest: An Indigenous Archaeology* (Berkeley: University of California Press, 2009), 11.

7. Wilcox, *The Pueblo Revolt*, 96.

MODULE 8
PLACE IN THE AUTHOR'S WORK

KEY POINTS

* Jared Diamond's three most famous books—*The Third Chimpanzee, Guns, Germs, and Steel*, and *Collapse*—are all about identifying the most important factors that drive change.
* All of Diamond's work is notable for its rigorous use of the "natural experiments"* of the comparative method.
* *Guns, Germs, and Steel* is Diamond's most famous book, and has been lauded with awards and translated into 36 languages.

Positioning

Although he is now much better known for his non-technical work, Jared Diamond was not always an author of popular books for a mass audience; his publications before *Guns, Germs, and Steel* were academic articles in specialist journals.

Diamond's first popular book—*The Third Chimpanzee*—was published in 1991. Like *Guns, Germs, and Steel*, it was a book intended for a general audience. Also, much like *Guns, Germs, and Steel*, it was concerned with how humanity came to dominate the world. In *The Third Chimpanzee*, Diamond focuses on the roots of human behavior in our evolutionary history. For example, he notes a "great leap forward" that occurred in the last 60,000 years involving the abrupt development of trade, culture, and (comparative) technological sophistication. This took place among anatomically modern humans, and Diamond suggests it was a result of the development of our ability to talk.[1] Language allowed humans to "brainstorm together about how to devise a better tool, or about what a cave painting might mean."[2]

Diamond's most significant work after *Guns, Germs, and Steel* was *Collapse: How Societies Choose to Fail or Survive* in 2005. While *The Third Chimpanzee* focused on evolution and *Guns, Germs, and Steel* focused on environments in which societies emerge, *Collapse* focused on what happens once societies are formed. By, "collapse," Diamond means "a drastic decrease in human population size and/or political, social, economic, or social complexity, over a considerable area, for an extended time."[3]

> "Of course it's not true that all societies are doomed to collapse because of environmental damage: in the past some societies did while others didn't; the real question is why only some societies proved fragile, and what distinguished those that collapsed from those that didn't."
>
> ——Jared Diamond, *Collapse*

Integration

What is distinctive about all of Diamond's work—especially the trilogy of *The Third Chimpanzee, Guns, Germs, and Steel*, and *Collapse*—is the scientific approach they share. For Diamond science is not defined as experiments in laboratory conditions,* but rather, "the acquisition of reliable knowledge about the world" in whatever way possible.[4] Moreover, in all his work, Diamond points his science in the same direction: the acquisition of reliable knowledge of the *long-term* factors, biological, environmental, and cultural, that have determined what the world looks like today, and what it may look like in future.

One of the key differences between Diamond's early work and *Collapse* is the importance of structure (the pattern of circumstances and institutions) and agency (independent choice) in shaping behavior. *Collapse* has a central role for human choice. Some societies, writes Diamond, succeeded in "solving extremely difficult environmental problems" by learning from experience and adapting their behavior to interact with their environments properly.This might be by controlling their populations, by finding new sources of food, or careful land management.[5] This is why Diamond includes the all-important word "choose" in the title of the book.

Collapse and *Guns, Germs, and Steel*, in particular, can be read as emphasizing two distinct factors (structure and agency) that have defined the development of human societies since prehistory. *Guns, Germs, and Steel* focuses on "buildups," whereas *Collapse* looks at the other end—shut down. Seeing Diamond's work as unified helps illustrate the explanatory power of taking a macro view—meaning focusing on the large scale and the long term—on societies to understand universal principles.

Significance

In all his writing, Diamond has demonstrated his ability to weave together information from a diverse spectrum of disciplines and explain it to a broad readership. He has won a popular following, including such public figures as the entrepreneur and philanthropist Bill Gates,* and has a role in ongoing debates over global development. With *Guns, Germs, and Steel* and its follow-up works, Diamond has increased his global reputation as an important voice with a unique integrated perspective of human history and ecology.

Much new information has become available since *Guns, Germs, and Steel* was first published, which Diamond claims has "enriched our understanding without fundamentally changing interpretations."[6] He stands by his main argument that continental environmental differences shaped the patterns of human history and he believes that the themes discussed in the text are still relevant to conversations about global development today.

Guns, Germs, and Steel made Jared Diamond a household name and continues to be the most widely recognized of his works. It has been adopted as a modern classic with a place in the coursework of many colleges and high schools around the world.

---

1. Jared Diamond, *The Rise and Fall of the Third Chimpanzee* (London: Vintage, 2002), 46.
2. Diamond, *The Rise and Fall of the Third Chimpanzee*, 47.
3. Jared Diamond, *Collapse: How Societies Choose to Fail or Survive* (London: Penguin, 2005), 3.
4. Diamond, *Collapse*, 17.
5. Diamond, *Collapse*, 10.
6. Jared Diamond, "Guns, Germs, and Steel: The Fates of Human Societies," accessed September 6, 2013, http://www.jareddiamond.org/Jared_ Diamond/Guns,_Germs,_and_Steel.html.

SECTION 3
IMPACT

THE FIRST RESPONSES

KEY POINTS

* Critics have argued that Diamond was wrong because his theory and its general assumptions "excuse" the crimes of European colonialism.*
* Diamond responds by suggesting that a scientific approach to history requires generalization.
* Diamond and his critics represent two opposing views of academia, what it should do and be, and the relative importance of scientific rigor.

Criticism

Jared Diamond's *Guns, Germs, and Steel* has been widely criticized for making many Eurocentric* assumptions (that is, it founds its arguments on ideas of European preeminence).

The American anthropologist James Blaut* argued that the book "is influential in part because its Eurocentric arguments seem, to a general reader, to be so compellingly 'scientific.'"[1] Blaut argues, largely, that Diamond has taken the way the world is today as inevitable—there was no other way history could go—and so he is attempting to justify it after the fact. Blaut's fundamental critique is of Diamond's explanation of the reasons Europe, rather than Eurasia generally, became globally dominant. He points out that the spread of technology is a key aspect of Eurasia's rise, until it comes to Europe's predominance.

The argument that "Europe had just the right balance between too little differentiation and too much" presents a problem because it means Diamond, based purely on a backward-looking justification of European dominance, is able to set his own boundary between "too little" and "too much."[2] In essence, Blaut's criticism of *Guns, Germs, and Steel* is that it was not a genuine attempt at a theory that could predict outcomes, but, rather, it made the existing distribution of power in the world look "natural."

The anthropologists Frederick Errington* and Deborah Gewertz* respond directly to Diamond in their 2004 book *Yali's Question*, named after the question posed by the New Guinean politician Yali* to Jared Diamond: "Why is it that you white people developed so much cargo and brought it to New Guinea, but we black people had little cargo of our own?"[3] "We find it problematic," they write, "that history's grand course can be adequately understood without considering culturally grounded ideas about what life is and might become."[4] Errington and Gewertz believe, in other words, that Diamond misunderstood Yali's question. Yali was not interested in the really great things that Western people invented. He was concerned about "Western condescension that allowed Europeans to deny Papua New Guineans fundamental worth."[5] In other words, Yali is questioning why Westerners hold all the power while New Guineans (and others in the developing world) are chronically disadvantaged. Diamond's answer, from this point of view, seems more like an excuse than an explanation—Westerners could not help conquering the world, and the resulting distribution of power is an inevitable consequence of geography.[6]

Ultimately, Errington and Gewertz's objection is about agency: just because one society *does* develop guns and steel, we should not conclude that they always conquer. The assumption that they will presupposes that all humans are self-regarding and acquisitive—but this is not a universal account of human nature. "Europeans had the resources and inclination to treat Yali and other Papua New Guineans with contempt," they write, but just because they could, does not mean they should be absolved.[7] In other words, individual choice must be brought back into the picture.

> "I dispute Diamond's argument not because he tries to use scientific data and scientific reasoning to solve the problems of human history.That is laudable. But he claims to produce reliable, scientific answers to these problems when in fact he does not have such answers, and he resolutely ignores the findings of social science while advancing old and discredited theories of environmental determinism.That is bad science."
>
> ——James Blaut, "Environmentalism and Eurocentrism"

Responses

Diamond's response to his critics was that they had misinterpreted his position—"our differences arise from the different historical scales that we consider."[8] In essence, Diamond's critics suggested that he did not leave enough space for culture and self-determination in his theory. His response to this was that the boundaries of what can be determined by culture are set by long-term history. Writing of the period following the last Ice Age,*

126

which ended some 12,000 years ago, he writes, "Over the hundreds of generations of post-Ice Age human history, and over a large continent's thousands of societies, cultural differences become sifted to approach limits imposed by environmental constraints."[9] Diamond is writing history from the most general perspective possible. Consequently, he needs to make some assumptions that underplay the role of individuals—but what he gains is the ability to describe universal trends.

Diamond suggests that the approach of his critics is effective for asking specific questions about specific events at specific times. One cannot say for sure why World War II* occurred when, where, and how it did without exploring the particulars of Germany's relationship with the rest of Europe and the Treaty of Versailles.* However, to ask questions of the widest generality—"Why was Europe so industrially advanced at the time of World War II compared to the rest of the world?" for example—one needs a theory that works on the widest of scales.

Conflict and Consensus

The debate between Diamond and his critics did not result in any positions shifting; they disagreed fundamentally about what academia is supposed to do and be. In essence, Diamond sees his academic mission as presenting a dispassionate, purely factual account of human history for 13,000 years. This means he denies agent-driven accounts (where societies are seen as the expression of different groups of people's independent choices), which do not necessarily purport to "rank" societies in order of their successful adaptation to structure. His critics, such as Errington and Gewertz, suggest he does not value societies that fail to become world-dominant, even though those societies may be the expression of the cultural preferences of those who live in them (e.g., that hunter-gatherer* tribes may value their lifestyles, and not see themselves as simply unlucky or failed).

This debate continues with Diamond's most recent work, *The World Until Yesterday*. In this book, he writes that "traditional societies represent thousands of millennia-long natural experiments in organizing human lives."[10] Canadian anthropologist Wade Davis's* review of the book criticized Diamond's inability to accept humanity's diversity; "the other peoples of the world are not failed attempts at modernity, let alone failed attempts to be us," he writes.[11] In other words, a tribe that either dies out or gets subsumed into another tribe represents two very different things for theorists like Diamond and Davis. For Diamond, they represent alternatives that did not work; for Davis, they represent the unique expression of those people's identity at that place and time. These points of view are both right. But they stem from fundamentally different—and mutually exclusive— perspectives.

1. James Blaut, "Environmentalism and Eurocentrism," *Geographical Review* 89, no. 3 (1999): 403.

2. Blaut, "Environmentalism and Eurocentrism," 403.

3. Jared M. Diamond, *Guns, Germs, and Steel: The Fates of Human Societies* (New York: W. W. Norton & Company, 1999), 14.

4. Frederick Errington and Deborah Gewrtz, *Yali's Question: Sugar, Culture, and History* (Chicago: University of Chicago Press, 2004), 7.

5. Errington and Gewrtz, *Yali's Question*, 8.

6. Errington and Gewrtz, *Yali's Question*, 9.

7. Errington and Gewertz. *Yali's Question*, 14.

8. Jared Diamond, "Guns, Germs, and Steel," *New York Review of Books*, June 26, 1997, accessed May 23, 2015, http://www.nybooks.com/articles/archives/1997/jun/26/guns-germs-and-steel/.

9. Diamond, "Guns, Germs, and Steel."

10. Jared Diamond, *The World Until Yesterday: What Can We Learn from Traditional Societies?* (London: Penguin, 2013), 32.

11. Wade Davis, "The World Until Yesterday by Jared Diamond: A Review," *Guardian*, January 9, 2013, accessed May 23, 2015, http://www. theguardian.com/books/2013/jan/09/history-society.

MODULE 10
THE EVOLVING DEBATE

KEY POINTS

* *Guns, Germs, and Steel* has become part of a scientific approach to economic development based on the search for laws and principles.

* The field of development economics compares a country's natural resources endowments with its chances of economic success.

* The writing of the American economist Jeffrey Sachs* is perhaps the most influential in this school of literature, especially Sachs's concept of the "resource curse."

Uses and Problems

Debates in geography, politics, and economics (especially economic development) turn on some of the points Diamond raises in *Guns, Germs, and Steel*, even if only implicitly. On the one hand, there is the mainstream "empiricist" or "positivist" approach; aiming to be scientific, with the use of statistics and technical information, it is an approach that makes generalizations and is associated with institutions like the World Bank.*[1] On the other hand, approaches that focus more on the role of ideas and culture sit outside the mainstream. They suggest that more "scientific" theories implicitly justify the domination of the developed world over the developing one and are "unwittingly invested in a set of persistent discourses that point to the need for change *over there*, rather than *over here*."[2]

There are key parallels between Diamond's 2005 book *Collapse* and the important United Nations* publication *A Guide to the World's Resources 2005*, for example. "It has long been suspected," Diamond writes, "[that societies collapse because] people inadvertently [destroyed]" the environmental resources on which their societies depended."[3] He suggests that the environmental problems that lead societies to collapse are "deforestation and habitat destruction, soil problems ... water management problems ... overhunting, overfishing, effects of introduced species on native species, human population growth, and increased per capita impact of people."[4]

Effectively, this is a list of the mistakes people make in their relationships with their environment. The *Resources* report opens by declaring that "[the] ecosystems of the world represent the natural capital stock of the planet," and "over the last 50 years, we have changed ecosystems more rapidly than at any time in human history, largely to meet growing demands for food, freshwater, timber, and fiber."[5] They suggest "this requires that the poor manage ecosystems so that they support stable productivity over time."[6] This idea—that environment, politics, and economic development are all connected, and that there is "one correct answer" to diagnose and solve the problem—is at one with Diamond's analysis, and continues to be important.

> "The livelihoods of the poor can be enhanced by capturing greater value from ecosystems. But this can only happen where good governance practices prevail. That means managing ecosystems sustainably and ensuring the poor access, voice, and participation. In other words, there is power in nature for poverty reduction, but only if we deal effectively with the nature of power—the governance over resources—so that the poor can reap the benefits of ecosystems."
> —— Gregory Mock, *A Guide to the World's Resources*

Schools of Thought

Diamond's work played an important role in helping define some of the problems historically tackled by economists who address developing economies.

In an article published in 1971, the development economist Paul Streeten* outlined the problem. The most striking fact of underdevelopment* today is that underdeveloped states "lie in the tropical* and semi-tropical zones," and that considering this a coincidence adds to the problem. He cites "a deep-seated optimistic bias with which we approach problems of development and the reluctance to admit the vast differences in initial conditions" faced by underdeveloped states.[7]

The American economist David Landes,* meanwhile, outlines a number of environmental conditions that lead to uneven development;* he focuses on the role of heat in encouraging more infectious disease and making work more difficult.[8]

One of the most important works in economic development to embrace Diamond's perspective of the relationship between geography and economic outcomes is by the economists John Gallup,* Jeffrey Sachs, and Andrew Mellinger.* In their survey of all the world's countries on the basis of their geographical situation and political history (for example, were they led by a dictator?), they looked at average income by nation. They found that "there are 23 countries with the most favored combination of geography and politics— Northern hemisphere, temperate* zone, coastal, non-war torn—with an average [income] of $18,000."[9] Being located in the tropics, not being located on a coast, being in the Southern hemisphere, and other similar criteria, were shown to reduce the predicted average income of a country by tens of thousands of dollars per capita.[10]

In Current Scholarship

Perhaps the most prominent thinker today who shares Diamond's point of view about the importance of the environment on human outcomes is the economist Jeffrey Sachs. In his article "Institutions Matter, but Not for Everything," Sachs argues that human factors (broadly defined as "institutions" and including everything from traditions to governments) account for only a part of economic development. Sachs distances himself from environmental determinism* (that is, the view that environmental factors decide everything as far as development is concerned), arguing that even if good health were "important to development," then an area climatically prone to malaria* will have special difficulties—but it will not be condemned to poverty forever.[11] Sachs concludes that environmental factors define the particular challenges states face in development. To imagine that all problems are either caused by "bad institutions" or by the exploitation of poor countries by rich countries ignores these important factors.[12]

One of the most important environmental factors Sachs identified (alongside the American economist Andrew Warner*) was the so-called "resource curse"—a phenomenon whereby countries with abundant natural resources, which should allow them to prosper economically, actually fail to develop or end up with very poor governance and social problems. There is currently no clear agreement on *how* the natural resource curse stops development, but one of Sachs and Warner's arguments is that, while the extraction and sale of abundant natural resources may generate income, it does not build a country's wider economy.[13] In other words, a country with oil can sell it in partnership with foreign oil companies and does not develop its own native industries. When the oil runs out, there are few native industries—such as those that export valuable, manufactured goods— to take over.

Unlike Diamond, Sachs is not interested in the consequences of 13,000 years of history, but the two share a key interest in how environmental conditions shape and constrain the choices societies make.

---

1. Maureen Hickey and Vicky Lawson, "Beyond Science? Human Geography, Interpretation, and Critique," in *Questioning Geography: Fundamental Debates*, ed. Noel Castree et al. (Malden, MA: Blackwell, 2005), 110.

2. Hickey and Lawson, "Beyond Science?" 109.

3. Jared M. Diamond, *Collapse: How Societies Choose to Fail or Survive* (London: Penguin, 2005), 4.

4. Diamond, *Collapse*, 4.

5. Gregory Mock, ed., *A Guide to World Resources 2005* (Washington, DC: World Resources Institute, 2005), 4.

6. Mock, *A Guide to World Resources*, 7.

7. Paul Streeten, "How Poor Are the Poor Countries?" in *Development in a Divided World*, ed. D. Seers and L. Joy (Harmondsworth: Penguin, 1971), 78.

8. David Landes, *The Wealth and Poverty of Nations: Why Some Are So Rich and Some Are So Poor* (New York: W. W. Norton & Company, 1998), 7–11.

9. John Gallup et al., *Geography and Economic Development* (Cambridge: National Bureau of Economic Research, 1998), 8.

10. Gallup et al., *Geography and Economic Development*, 8.

11. Jeffrey Sachs, "Institutions Matter, but Not for Everything," *Finance and Development* 40, no. 2 (June 2003): 40.

12. Sachs, "Institutions Matter, but Not for Everything," 38–9.

13. Jeffrey Sachs and Andrew Warner, "The Curse of Natural Resources," *European Economic Review* 45, nos. 4–6 (2001): 833.

MODULE 11
IMPACT AND INFLUENCE TODAY

KEY POINTS

• *Guns, Germs, and Steel* is less directly relevant today than other works that share its scientific methodology (especially in economic development).

• The Canadian economist Nathan Nunn,* for example, argues that there is a strong correlation between the number of slaves taken from certain parts of Africa and current levels of underdevelopment.*

• Critics of this method suggest it is oversimplistic and ignores complex factors such as relationships of dominance, which can determine outcomes more than any "underlying" factor.

Position

Jared Diamond's *Guns, Germs, and Steel* occupies a prominent place on undergraduate reading lists in international history, politics, economics, geography, sociology, and numerous other disciplines. This is, in part, because it is so well written, popular, and accessible.

From an academic standpoint, however, the book is on shakier ground. For example, the American historian Stephen Wertheim,* in a review of *The World Until Yesterday*, wrote, "*Guns, Germs, and Steel* attacked the notion that racial superiority explained Western global pre-eminence, a view taken seriously by almost no one who's taken seriously."[1] The economists Daron Acemoglu* and James Robinson's* influential *Why Nations Fail* takes a more charitable approach: *Guns, Germs, and Steel* "cannot be extended to explain modern world inequality" because it simplifies too much, meaning it cannot address why "the average Spaniard is more than six times richer than the average Peruvian," and how to rectify the situation.[2]

Guns, Germs, and Steel is now more relevant for its use of "comparative methodology"* on the grandest of scales (an approach that aims to figure out the effects of given factors on given outcomes by examining two or more cases, their similarities and differences). In *Natural Experiments of History*, a volume Diamond co-edited with the British political theorist James Robinson,* Diamond expanded on this idea and explored its possible uses. "Historical comparisons," the book concludes, "may yield insights that cannot be extracted from a single case study alone" and "when one proposes a conclusion, one may be able to strengthen that conclusion [by using empirical evidence]."[3]

So, why does *Guns, Germs, and Steel* still matter? In part, because it is an accessible and intellectually graspable introduction to the comparative method for undergraduates. As we have seen, perhaps it is for its methodology, more than its conclusions, that it remains so widely read among academics.

> "Why are the institutions of the United States so much more conducive to economic success than those of Mexico, or for that matter, the rest of Latin America? The answer to this question lies in the way different societies formed during the early colonial* period. An institutional divergence took place then, with implications lasting into the present day. To understand this divergence we must begin right at the foundation of the colonies in North and Latin America."
>
> —— Daron Acemoglu and James Robinson, *Why Nations Fail*

Interaction

The challenge Diamond and his fellow scientists of history pose today tends to focus on the difference between cultural anthropology and science.

The economist Nathan Nunn, for example, contributed the chapter "Shackled to the Past: The Causes and Consequences of Africa's Slave Trades" to Diamond and Robinson's *Natural Experiments of History*. In it, Nunn found that the "parts of the continent from which the largest number of slaves were taken in the past are the parts of the continent that are the poorest today."[4] What is most striking about Nunn's findings is the extent of their scientific rigor; Nunn uses "statistical analysis to examine the relationship between the severity of the slave trades and subsequent economic performance for different parts of Africa."[5] His analysis of the slave trade in Africa is large scale— he makes generalizations that mean the experience of, for example, areas that comprise modern Zimbabwe and the Congo are compared as though they are similar.

Finding a balance between generality and specificity is a serious challenge. Anyone would admit that different areas would have had different experiences of the slave trade. But natural experiments like Nunn's can show that a few common factors—the intensity of the slave trade, for example—have significant power to explain the current conditions of many different peoples.

The Continuing Debate

In the book *Questioning Collapse*, the American anthropologists

Patricia McAnany* and Norman Yoffee* bring together a number of responses to Diamond.

The American anthropologists Frederick Errington* and Deborah Gewertz,* meanwhile, updating their arguments from their book *Yali's Question*, which criticizes Diamond's *Guns, Germs, and Steel*, contribute the essay "Excusing the Haves and Blaming the Have Nots in the Telling of History." In it, they argue that "basing history on what appear to be commonsense (Western) suppositions, makes complex political processes into simple, inevitable laws." And basing history on "laws" then makes the current state of affairs look natural.[6]

The problem, they claim, is that this view of history means we do not consider the brutality of the conquistadors* as morally wrong. Factors beyond their control (Eurasian geography and the distribution of plant and animal life) meant the Spanish could not have helped themselves, and the Andean people were doomed from the outset. This is a rejection of the themes that unite *Collapse* and *Guns, Germs, and Steel*. Their argument is that in *Collapse*, Diamond assumes every society "will have an equal capacity to choose"—from cultural factors, to abuse from outside powers, to simply bad luck. For them, this assumption ultimately "clouds our understanding of the processes actually affecting the world today."[7]

Errington and Gewertz give the example of the sugar industries in the United States and Papua New Guinea. The United States subsidizes* its own sugar production (that is, it spends public money to make sure that their sugar is cheap on the open market). "Papua New Guinea's government," on the other hand, "is heavily

pressured by the World Bank* and the World Trade Organization"*
to be uncompetitive on the open market.[8] This means they cannot
subsidize their own sugar industry, nor are they allowed to impose
import taxes (called "tariffs") on American sugar. It is not clear
how this state of affairs is a result of Papua New Guinea's choices,
nor is it clear how the power of the United States in international
trade is excusable because it arises from a historical inevitability.

1. Stephen Wertheim, "Hunter-Blatherer," *The Nation*, April 22, 2013, 37.

2. Daron Acemoglu and James Robinson, *Why Nations Fail: The Origins of Power, Prosperity, and Poverty* (London: Profile Books, 2012), 52.

3. Jared Diamond and James Robinson, "Afterword," in *Natural Experiments of History*, ed. Jared Diamond and James Robinson (Cambridge, MA: Harvard University Press, 2010), 274.

4. Nathan Nunn, "Shackled to the Past: The Causes and Consequences of Africa's Slave Trades," in *Natural Experiments of History*, ed. Jared Diamond and James Robinson (Cambridge, MA: Harvard University Press, 2010), 142.

5. Nunn, "Shackled to the Past," 146.

6. Frederick Errington and Deborah Gewertz, "Excusing the Haves and Blaming the Have Nots in the Telling of History," in *Questioning Collapse: Human Resilience, Ecological Vulnerability, and the Aftermath of Empire*, ed. Patricia McAnany and Norman Yoffee (Cambridge: Cambridge University Press, 2009), 329–51, 330.

7. Errington and Gewertz, "Excusing the Haves," 341.

8. Errington and Gewertz, "Excusing the Haves," 348–9.

MODULE 12
WHERE NEXT?

KEY POINTS

* *Guns, Germs, and Steel* cemented Diamond's reputation as a public intellectual and he has applied his approach to contemporary problems.
* As Diamond focuses more on culture and methodology, the Anglo-American historian Ian Morris* has taken up the task of explaining *longue durée* history.
* *Guns, Germs, and Steel* provided a scientifically rigorous explanation for the difficult problem of international inequality.

Potential

Jared Diamond's *Guns, Germs, and Steel* is unlikely to continue being influential in itself—the arguments are not generally taken seriously by other anthropologists or sociologists, who consider it to be either mistaken in its facts, or mistaken in its overall mission to do history as science. *Guns, Germs, and Steel* did, however, help to popularize the comparative method* in history.

Diamond's current work with development economists, looking at shorter time-scales and more specific problems, continues to be important."What is going to happen in the United States?" Diamond asks in a recent article, in the context of declining global prominence and mounting budgetary pressure.[1]

Having restated his argument that political competition moves ideas and development forward, while allowing bad ideas (the abolition of the navy, for example, or the destruction of the middle class) to fail.[2]

Diamond notes four threats to this good state of affairs: political compromise has been declining; there are increasing restrictions on the right to vote; there is a growing gap between the rich and the poor; and, finally, there are too few opportunities to develop intellectual capital[*3] (that is, the nation's wealth of ideas, technology, and innovation). Diamond concludes this means the US will slowly lose the competitive advantages it has accumulated.

> *"Both long-termers and short-termers agree that the West has dominated the globe for the last two hundred years, but disagree over what the world was like before this. Everything revolves around their differing assumptions of premodern history.The only way we can resolve this dispute is by looking at these earlier periods to establish the overall 'shape' of history."*
>
> —— Ian Morris, *Why the West Rules—For Now*

Future Directions

Diamond has written increasingly about culture (*The World Until Yesterday*) and methodology (*Natural Experiments of History*). The classical historian Ian Morris, however, has written two books recently that push the *Guns, Germs, and Steel* hypothesis forward.

His book *Why the West Rules—For Now:The Patterns of History and What They Reveal About the Future* (2010) attempts to bridge the gap between long- and short-term approaches to global history."We will not find answers," Morris writes,"if we restrict our search to prehistory or modern times." Instead, historians ought to "look at the whole sweep of human history as a single story, establishing its overall shape."[4] Whereas Diamond argues that only the very earliest factors matter as causes (everything else is just a knock-on effect), Morris believes "ultimate" causes can emerge throughout history: "Western rule was neither predetermined thousands of years ago nor a result of recent accidents."[5]

The key concept of Morris's work is "social development," which he takes to mean "a group's ability to master its physical and intellectual environment to 'get things done' ... the bundle of technological, subsistence, organizational, and cultural accomplishments" through which people understand and manage the natural and social worlds.[6]

Morris concludes that geography and "social development" determine the shape of history, and constantly redefine one another, writing that "geography determined where in the world social development would rise fastest, but rising social development changes what geography meant."[7] Britain may have lost out on the spread of technology that occurred in Europe after the medieval period, for example, being an island off the continent, but when having powerful navies became important for global domination, then Britain's position on the Atlantic was a major advantage in developing its empire.

Summary

Jared Diamond's *Guns, Germs, and Steel* was both a timely and a controversial book. He aimed to present a view of history that went beyond simple, obvious explanations of why the world is the way it is—and particularly why "the West" is so powerful. He dismisses answers that look only at the obvious, "proximate" causes, which would explain Western domination by its superior technology or singular forms of government, because they tell only part of the story. He prefers to dig deeper, looking for "ultimate" causes: If technology is key to dominating the world, why, then, did the West develop better technology?

To make his arguments, Diamond looks to archaeology to examine the first divergences between groups that would become the complex societies in which technology develops and those societies that remains as hunter-gatherers,* where complex technology does not develop. The key difference was *agriculture*. Societies that become agricultural can have specialist rulers, scientists, blacksmiths, and scribes. Looking for ultimate causes, Diamond goes back a step further: why do some societies develop agriculture, and others do not? Random geographical factors determine the presence of plants and animals that are well suited to domestication.* For Diamond, this inevitably led to agriculture, which led to society, which led to "guns, germs, and steel"—and eventually Western global dominance.

---

1. Jared Diamond, "Four Threats to American Democracy," *Governance* 27, no. 2 (2014): 189.

2. Diamond, "Four Threats to American Democracy," 186.

3. Diamond, "Four Threats to American Democracy," 186–7.

4. Ian Morris, *Why the West Rules—For Now: The Patterns of History and What They Reveal About the Future* (New York: Farrar, Straus and Giroux, 2010), 22.

5. Morris, *Why The West Rules*, 25.

6. Morris, *Why The West Rules*, 144.

7. Morris, *Why The West Rules*, 35.

GLOSSARY OF TERMS

1. **Annales school:** a historical school of thought that emphasizes the long-term influences on day-to-day living, rather than dramatic events.

2. **Cajamarca:** a major city in Peru. It was also the site of a major battle between Spanish conquistadors and native Incas.

3. **Capitalism:** an economic system in which most industrial activity (but not necessarily all) is controlled by private owners, for profit.

4. **Cold War (1947–91):** a period of tension between the United States and the Soviet Union, and their allies. While the two blocs never engaged in direct military conflict, they engaged in covert and proxy wars and espionage.

5. **Colonialism:** the invasion and establishment of a colony in a target territory by a central state. It is characterized by a deeply unequal relationship between the native and colonizing populations.

6. **Comparative method:** involves examining two cases and identifying the underlying factors that have driven their respective outcomes.

7. **Conquistadors:** a term used to describe Spanish and Portuguese explorers and soldiers who simultaneously "discovered" and conquered lands in the Americas, Oceania, and even parts of Asia, especially between the fifteenth and seventeenth centuries.

8. **Despotism:** a form of government that invests all authority in one individual or group of individuals.

9. **Domestication:** refers to the process by which humans use selective breeding in order to encourage or discourage certain traits that make the organism more useful.

10. **Empiricism:** a theory of knowledge. It holds that knowledge comes only from what one can observe.

11. **Environmental determinism:** the idea that factors in an environment "lock in" given historical trajectories. It is an extreme form of structuralism, because it has no space for agency (that is, the potential of individuals to change circumstances through action).

12. **Eurocentrism:** a criticism of many Western social scientific theories. The criticism is that these theories make many assumptions that Europeans would make, especially about the natural superiority of Europe and European ideas, which members of other cultures do not see as natural.

13. **Globalization:** the process of increasing interconnectedness around the globe, driven by improvements in travel, shipping, and telecommunications, among other technologies.

14. **Hunter-gatherer community:** a small group of humans that relies on wild sources of food (hunting, rather than raising animals, and gathering, rather than farming, plants). Societies organized along these lines tend to move frequently and to devote much time to food procurement.

15. **Ice Age:** a reduction in the temperature of the Earth's surface over a long period of time. During an Ice Age, most of North America and Europe would be covered by glacier ice.The last Ice Age ended some 12,500 years ago.

16. **Intellectual capital:** roughly, the value of ideas, knowledge, and innovation.

17. **Laboratory conditions:** refers to the careful, controlled environment of a laboratory, where a phenomenon can be studied without interference from the outside world.

18. *Longue durée*: a French phrase meaning "long term," and referring, in the context of history, to the approach taken by the historians of the Annales school, concerned with historical changes (often social changes) over the long term.

19. **Ludwig von Mises Institute:** a think tank from the United States that promotes lower levels of government interference in daily life. It is named after Austrian economist Ludwig von Mises, who was skeptical of the government's ability to plan more effectively than the free market.

20. **Malaria:** a disease caused by a parasite carried in mosquitoes. It only appears in warm, wet areas of the world. Over 600,000 people died of malaria in 2010.

21. **Man-land geography:** one of the four major traditions of geography, emphasizing how the environment and people mutually affect one another.

22. **Natural experiments:** these occur, usually by luck, when two groups of

individuals who are mostly similar are exposed to two different conditions. Researchers can infer what one condition does to one group, relative to another.

23. **Natural selection:** the process, first described by Charles Darwin, whereby some traits in organisms affect the reproductive success of that organism under given conditions, and those traits thereby become more or less prevalent.

24. **Parsimony:** refers to the principle that a theory should make predictions as simply as possible, using as few factors as necessary.

25. **Processual archaeology:** a school of thought in archaeology that suggests archaeology should seek to use physical evidence of the past in order to reconstruct what life was genuinely like. It aims to establish "laws" of human behavior based on commonalities between cultures.

26. **Pulitzer Prize:** a highly prestigious American award for excellence in newspaper and online journalism, as well as literature and musical composition.

27. **Stone Age:** refers to two separate, related things. It refers to an era of prehistory that was characterized by the use of stone tools by humans, ending between 6000 and 3000 B.C.E. It also refers to levels of technological development that still exist among some scattered hunter-gatherer tribes.

28. **Structuralism:** a way of seeing the world in social sciences that emphasizes the causal role of external conditions in shaping human action. It is often opposed to agency, which emphasizes the causal role of individual motivation.

29. **Subsidy:** a form of financial support extended (usually by a government) to a sector of the economy, in order to make it more competitive.

30. **Temperate climates:** these exist between the warm tropical regions and the cold arctic regions of the Earth. Temperate climates are characterized by four seasons, with moderate temperatures.

31. **Treaty of Versailles (1919):** refers to the peace treaty signed between the Allied Powers and a defeated Germany at the end of World War I. It has historically been criticized for being too punitive on Germany, and contributing to the degradation of its already fragile economy.

32. **Tropical climates:** these tend to cluster near the equator and are characterized

by year-round warmth.

33. **Underdevelopment:** a condition that is experienced by states that are not using their resources to their full productive potential.

34. **Uneven development:** refers to the process whereby different areas develop economically at different rates.

35. **United Nations:** a supra-governmental organization headquartered in NewYork City comprising nearly every state in the world. Its most important functions include overseeing global security matters and promoting global cooperation.

36. **World Bank:** an international institution based in Washington, DC. It offers loans and advice to countries that require development assistance.

37. **World-systems theory:** an approach to world sociology and history that turns on the idea that some countries are systematically exploited by others.

38. **World Trade Organization:** an international institution based in Geneva, Switzerland. It regulates trade between countries, and attempts to ensure it is fair and open.

39. **World War II (1939–45):** a global conflict fought between the Axis Powers (Germany, Italy, and Japan) and the victorious Allied Powers (United Kingdom and its colonies and dominions, the former Soviet Union, and the United States).

PEOPLE MENTIONED IN THE TEXT

1. **Daron Acemoglu (b. 1967)** is a Turkish American development economist. He and the economist James Robinson famously take an "institutions" approach to development, meaning states with "good" institutions (non-extractive, fair, and so on) will out-develop states with "bad" institutions.

2. **Atahuallpa (1500–33)** was an Incan emperor. Atahuallpa was captured by the Spanish in 1532, and was briefly imprisoned before being executed.

3. **James Blaut (1927–2000)** was professor of anthropology at the University of Illinois at Chicago. Blaut's career was characterized by the exposure of Eurocentric biases in mainstream history.

4. **Fernand Braudel (1902–85)** was a French historian, and key figure in the Annales school. He is notable for emphasizing the role of large-scale, long-term socio-economic shifts in driving history (rather than the decisions of kings).

5. **Gene Callahan (b. 1959)** is an American economist. Callahan argues in favor of reliance on the free market, rather than central planning.

6. **William Catton (1929–2015)** was an American sociologist. He is notable as one of the founders of environmental sociology, which was one of the first forms of sociology to look beyond purely social factors.

7. **Christopher Columbus (1451–1506)** was an Italian explorer. Looking for an alternative route to India, Columbus famously sailed from Europe, across the Atlantic, to America in 1492.

8. **Alfred Crosby (1931–2018)** was an American historian and geographer. He was famous for his book *The Colombian Exchange*, which explores the effect of the separation of Earth's two major landmasses coming to an abrupt halt in 1492 with the voyage of Columbus.

9. **Charles Darwin (1809–82)** was a British naturalist, famous for setting out the theory of evolution by natural selection.

10. **Wade Davis (b. 1953)** is a Canadian anthropologist and naturalist. His work emphasizes the differences between different cultures, and a rejection of any idea that one culture can be called superior to another.

11. **Riley Dunlap** is an American sociologist at Oklahoma State University. Along with William Catton, Dunlap is famous for setting out the environmental theory of sociology.

12. **Frederick Errington** is distinguished professor of anthropology at Trinity College, Connecticut. His work with Deborah Gewertz emphasizes themes of economics and culture, complex theories of change, and the importance of multiple perspectives in understanding all of the above.

13. **John Gallup (b. 1962)** is an American development economist. He has published numerous papers on the influence of different geographic factors on development outcomes.

14. **Bill Gates (b. 1955)** is an American entrepreneur and philanthropist, and has occupied the top of the world's rich list. He made his fortune founding Microsoft, but now supports economic development through the Bill and Melinda Gates Foundation.

15. **Deborah Gewertz** is professor of anthropology at Amherst College in Massachusetts. Her work with the anthropologist Frederick Errington emphasizes themes of economics and culture, complex theories of change, and the importance of multiple perspectives in understanding all of the above.

16. **David Humphreys** is a British professor of social policy at Green Templeton College at the University of Oxford.

17. **Ellsworth Huntington (1876–1947)** was an American geographer. He is known for his theory of geographic determinism.

18. **Mark D. Jacobs** is professor of sociology at George Mason University in the United States. Studying trends in the discipline of sociology is one of his key research interests, but he has also studied the sociology of finance.

19. **Eric Jones (b. 1936)** is a British Australian economic historian. His book *The European Miracle* sought to explain why industrial productivity was so high in Europe.

20. **David Landes (1924–2013)** was an American professor of economics and history at Harvard University.

21. **Philip Mancus** is professor of psychology and sociology at the College of the Redwoods in the United States. His work focuses on human behavior.

22. **Patricia McAnany (b. 1963)** is an American anthropologist who specializes in the history and archaeology of the Mayan civilization in the Americas.

23. **Andrew Mellinger** is an American economist who is known for his writing on the relation between development economics and geography.

24. **Ian Morris (b. 1960)** is an Anglo-American historian, specializing in classics. He specializes in long-term history, and his recent work focuses on the role of warfare in economic development.

25. **Nathan Nunn** is a Canadian professor of economics at Harvard University. He is well known for his work on economic history, especially with relation to development.

26. **William D. Pattison (1921–97)** was an American geographer at the University of Chicago. He is well known not only for his work on geography as a discipline, but also in patterns of land use in the United States.

27. **Francisco Pizarro (c. 1471–1541)** was a Spanish colonial commander. He commanded the forces that conquered the Incan empire. He became the first governor of the Spanish territories in what is now Peru in 1528.

28. **James Robinson (b. 1960)** is a British economist and political theorist at Harvard University. His work with Daron Acemoglu in development economics, *Why Nations Fail*, is known for emphasizing the role of policy and institutions.

29. **Jeffrey Sachs (b. 1954)** is an American economist at Harvard University. He focuses on sustainable development, especially regarding the environment. He was involved in the creation of the United Nations Millennium Development Goals.

30. **Lyn Spillman** is professor of sociology at the University of Notre Dame in the US. Her work examines the influence of social forces on political strategy.

31. **Julien Steward (1902–72)** was an American anthropologist. His research focused on the ways in which humanity manipulates our natural environment to sustain ourselves.

32. **Paul Streeten (1917–2019)** was an Anglo-Austrian American development economist. He was known for outlining the "basic needs" approach to development, and advising the British Ministry of Overseas Development in the 1960s.

33. **Stuart Vyse** is professor of psychology at Connecticut College. He specializes in the analysis of behavior.

34. **Immanuel Wallerstein (b. 1930)** is an American sociologist, best known for promoting world-systems theory. The theory states that there is a division of labor between the developed "core" states (the West, primarily) and peripheral states. The core uses the periphery to extract resources and labor for its own benefit.

35. **Andrew Warner** is an American economist. He is concerned with theorizing how and why governments invest in their own development.

36. **Stephen Wertheim** is a young American historian. He wrote his review of Diamond in the journal *Nation* while still a graduate student at Columbia University.

37. **Michael Wilcox** is an associate professor of anthropology at Stanford University in the US. His research interests focus on the history of the native populations of the Southwestern United States.

38. **Yali (1912–75)** was a Papua New Guinean politician and activist. His political career involved mediating relationships between the central government and the native communities.

39. **Norman Yoffee** is professor of anthropology and Near Eastern studies at New York University. He is particularly interested in ancient Mesopotamia, and what factors prompted ancient states to rise and fall.

40. **Richard York** is professor of sociology and environmental studies at the University of Oregon. His work focuses on climate change and human impact on the environment.

WORKS CITED

1. Acemoglu, Daron, and James Robinson. *Why Nations Fail: The Origins of Power, Prosperity, and Poverty*. London: Profile Books, 2012.

2. Blaut, James. "Environmentalism and Eurocentrism." *Geographical Review* 89, no. 3 (1999): 391–408.

3. Braudel, Fernand. *The Mediterranean World in the Age of Philip II: Volume I*. London: University of California Press, 1995.

4. Callahan, Gene. "The Diamond Fallacy," Mises Institute. Accessed May 17, 2015. https://mises.org/library/diamond-fallacy.

5. Crosby, Alfred W. *The Colombian Exchange: Biological and Cultural Consequences of 1492*. Westport, CT: Praeger, 2003.

6. Darwin, Charles. *On the Origin of Species*. Oxford: Oxford University Press, 2008.

7. Davis, Wade. "*The World Until Yesterday* by Jared Diamond: A Review." *Guardian*, January 9, 2013. Accessed May 23, 2015. http://www.theguardian.com/books/2013/jan/09/history-society.

8. Diamond, Jared. "Guns, Germs, and Steel." *New York Review of Books*, June 26, 1997. Accessed May 23, 2015. http://www.nybooks.com/articles/archives/1997/jun/26/guns-germs-and-steel/.

9. ——. *Guns, Germs, and Steel: The Fates of Human Societies*. New York: W. W. Norton & Company, 1999.

10. ——. *The Rise and Fall of the Third Chimpanzee*. London: Vintage, 2002.

11. ——. *Collapse: How Societies Choose to Fail or Survive*. London: Penguin, 2005.

12. ——. "Guns, Germs, and Steel: The Fates of Human Societies." Accessed September 6, 2013. http://www.jareddiamond.org/Jared_Diamond/Guns,_Germs,_and_Steel.html.

13. ——. *The World Until Yesterday: What Can We Learn from Traditional Societies?* London: Penguin, 2013.

14. ——. "Four Threats to American Democracy." *Governance* 27, no. 2 (2014):

185–9.

15. ——. "About Me." Accessed May 30, 2015. http://www.jareddiamond.org/Jared_Diamond/About_Me.html.

16. Diamond, Jared, and James Robinson. "Afterword." In *Natural Experiments of History*. Edited by Jared Diamond and James Robinson, 142–75. Cambridge, MA: Harvard University Press, 2010.

17. Dunlap, Riley, and William Catton. "Environmental Sociology." *Annual Review of Sociology* 5 (1979): 243–73.

18. Earle, Timothy K., and Robert W. Preucel. "Processual Archaeology and the Radical Critique." *Current Anthropology* 28, no. 4 (1987): 501–38.

19. Errington, Frederick, and Deborah Gewertz. *Yali's Question: Sugar, Culture, and History*. Chicago: University of Chicago Press, 2004.

20. ——. "Excusing the Haves and Blaming the Have Nots in the Telling of History." In *Questioning Collapse: Human Resilience, Ecological Vulnerability, and the Aftermath of Empire*. Edited by Patricia McAnany and Norman Yoffee, 329–51. Cambridge: Cambridge University Press, 2009.

21. Gallup, John, Jeffrey Sachs, and Andrew Mellinger. *Geography and Economic Development*. Cambridge: National Bureau of Economic Research, 1998.

22. Hickey, Maureen, and Vicky Lawson. "Beyond Science? Human Geography, Interpretation, and Critique." In *Questioning Geography: Fundamental Debates*. Edited by Noel Castree, Alisdair Rogers, and Douglas Sherman, 96–115. Malden, MA: Blackwell, 2005.

23. Hippocrates. *On Airs, Waters, and Places*. Translated by Francis Adams. Accessed May 2, 2015. http://classics.mit.edu/Hippocrates/airwatpl.1.1.html.

24. Humphreys, David K., Manuel P. Eisner, and Douglas J. Wiebe. "Evaluating the Impact of Flexible Alcohol Trading Hours on Violence: An Interrupted Time Series Analysis." *PLOS ONE* 8, no. 2 (2013). Accessed July 15, 2015. doi:10.1371/journal.pone.0055581.

25. Huntington, Ellsworth. *Civilization and Climate*. New Haven, CT: Yale

University Press, 1915.

26. Jacobs, Mark D., and Lyn Spillman. "Cultural Sociology at the Crossroads of a Discipline." *Poetics* 33 (2005): 1–14.

27. Jones, Eric. *The European Miracle: Environments, Economies, and Geopolitics in the History of Europe and Asia*. Cambridge: Cambridge University Press, 2003.

28. Landes, David. *The Wealth and Poverty of Nations: Why Some Are So Rich and Some Are So Poor*. New York: W. W. Norton & Company, 1998.

29. McKie, Robin. "Jared Diamond: What We Can Learn from Tribal Life." *Guardian*, January 6, 2013. Accessed July 15, 2015. http://www.theguardian.com/ science/2013/jan/06/jared-diamond-tribal-life-anthropology.

30. Miller, Christopher. "Review of *Guns, Germs, and Steel: The Fate of Human Societies*, by Jared Diamond." *Economic Botany* 56, no. 2 (2002): 209.

31. Mock, Gregory. *A Guide to World Resources 2005*. Washington, DC: World Resources Institute, 2005.

32. Morris, Ian. *Why the West Rules—For Now: The Patterns of History and What They Reveal About the Future*. New York: Farrar, Straus and Giroux, 2010.

33. Nunn, Nathan. "Shackled to the Past: The Causes and Consequences of Africa's Slave Trades." In *Natural Experiments of History*. Edited by Jared Diamond and James Robinson, 142–84. Cambridge, MA: Harvard University Press, 2010.

34. Pattison, William. "The Four Traditions of Geography." *Journal of Geography* 63, no. 5 (1964): 211–16.

35. Sachs, Jeffrey. "Institutions Matter, but Not for Everything." *Finance and Development* 40, no. 2 (June 2003): 38–41.

36. Sachs Jeffrey, and Andrew Warner. "The Curse of Natural Resources." *European Economic Review* 45, no. 4–6 (2001): 827–38.

37. Sluyter, Andrew. "Neo-Environmental Determinism, Intellectual Damage Control, and Nature/Society Science." *Antipode* 35, no. 4 (2003): 813–17.

38. Steward, Julien. *Theory of Culture Change: The Methodology of Multilinear*

Evolution. Chicago: University of Illinois Press, 1972.

39. Streeten, Paul. "How Poor Are the Poor Countries?" In *Development in a Divided World.* Edited by D. Seers and L. Joy, 67–83. Harmondsworth: Penguin, 1971.

40. ul-Haq, Mahbub, ed. *Human Development Report 1990.* New York: Oxford University Press, 1990.

41. Vyse, Stuart. "World History for Behavior Analysts: Jared Diamond's *Guns, Germs, and Steel.*" *Behavior and Social Issues* 11, no. 1 (2001): 80–7.

42. Wallerstein, Immanuel. *The Modern World System I: Capitalist Agriculture and the Origins of the European World Economy in the Sixteenth Century.* London: University of California Press, 2011.

43. Wertheim, Stephen. "Hunter-Blatherer." *The Nation,* April 22, 2013.

44. Wilcox, Michael. *The Pueblo Revolt and the Mythology of Conquest: An Indigenous Archaeology.* Berkeley, CA: University of California Press, 2009.

45. ———. "Marketing Conquest and the Vanishing Indian: An Indigenous Response to Jared Diamond's *Guns, Germs, and Steel.*" *Journal of Social Archaeology* 10, no. 1 (2010): 92–117.

46. York, Richard, and Philip Mancus. "Diamond in the Rough: Reflections on *Guns, Germs, and Steel.*" *Research in Human Ecology* 14, no. 2 (2007): 157–62.

原书作者简介

贾雷德·M.戴蒙德1937年出生于美国波士顿，主要研究方向为人类历史，擅长跨学科研究，所涉领域包括生物学、人类学、生态学和地理学等。他先后分别在哈佛大学和剑桥大学攻读生物化学、生理学专业，1964年前往新几内亚时又对生态学产生兴趣。戴蒙德后来又研究过环境史，现任加利福尼亚大学洛杉矶分校地理学教授，同时也是环保主义者和畅销书作家。1998年，他曾凭借《枪炮、病菌与钢铁：人类社会的命运》一书荣获普利策奖。

本书作者简介

赖利·奎恩，伦敦政治经济学院、牛津大学政治学与国际关系专业双硕士。

世界名著中的批判性思维

《世界思想宝库钥匙丛书》致力于深入浅出地阐释全世界著名思想家的观点，不论是谁、在何处都能了解到，从而推进批判性思维发展。

《世界思想宝库钥匙丛书》与世界顶尖大学的一流学者合作，为一系列学科中最有影响的著作推出新的分析文本，介绍其观点和影响。在这一不断扩展的系列中，每种选入的著作都代表了历经时间考验的思想典范。通过为这些著作提供必要背景、揭示原作者的学术渊源以及说明这些著作所产生的影响，本系列图书希望让读者以新视角看待这些划时代的经典之作。读者应学会思考、运用并挑战这些著作中的观点，而不是简单接受它们。

ABOUT THE AUTHOR OF THE ORIGINAL WORK

Born in Boston in the United States in 1937, Jared M. Diamond studies human history using a wide-ranging approach that draws on biology, anthropology, ecology, and geography. He first trained as a biochemist at Harvard University and as a physiologist at Cambridge University, but became interested in ecology when he visited New Guinea in 1964. He then developed an interest in environmental history, and is now professor of geography at the University of California, Los Angeles, as well as an environmental activist and popular writer. He won the prestigious Pulitzer Prize for his 1997 work *Guns, Germs, and Steel: The Fates of Human Societies.*

ABOUT THE AUTHOR OF THE ANALYSIS

Riley Quinn holds master's degrees in politics and international relations from both LSE and the University of Oxford.

ABOUT MACAT
GREAT WORKS FOR CRITICAL THINKING

Macat is focused on making the ideas of the world's great thinkers accessible and comprehensible to everybody, everywhere, in ways that promote the development of enhanced critical thinking skills.

It works with leading academics from the world's top universities to produce new analyses that focus on the ideas and the impact of the most influential works ever written across a wide variety of academic disciplines. Each of the works that sit at the heart of its growing library is an enduring example of great thinking. But by setting them in context — and looking at the influences that shaped their authors, as well as the responses they provoked — Macat encourages readers to look at these classics and game-changers with fresh eyes. Readers learn to think, engage and challenge their ideas, rather than simply accepting them.

批判性思维与《枪炮、病菌与钢铁》

首要批判性思维技巧：理性化思维

次要批判性思维技巧：阐释

1997 年，《枪炮、病菌与钢铁：人类社会的命运》一书出版。贾雷德·M.戴蒙德在书中整合了横跨五大洲、贯穿人类 13 000 年历史的样本和案例，只为解答一个谜题：历史缘何在世界各地有着截然不同的发展结果。这本书还为我们当今所面临的社会问题提供了新颖的解读视角：世界权力和财富分配的不均衡是如何形成的，又为何持续下来。

《枪炮、病菌与钢铁》广泛汲取并权衡了来自各个学科的多种样本和案例，剖析了历史学家、人类学家、生物学家和地理学家所关心的重要问题，并将诸多论证糅合整理，生发出了引人入胜、颇具说服力的叙述模式，进而成为一本畅销全球、广受读者认可和欢迎的现象级图书。这些都需要作者具备极强的批判思维能力，鲜有学者能与之匹敌。出色的推理论证能力，令读者心悦诚服于他的跨学科研究方法，也让戴蒙德能够清晰地组织和表达一系列论点，从一个案例过渡到另一段与之毫不相干的叙述，带领读者饶有兴味地逐页阅读。

戴蒙德还具备另一种出色的能力，他能够整合运用来自不同学科和不同学者的已有论据，让《枪炮、病菌与钢铁》也成为一本蕴含深刻见解的、有价值的书。

CRITICAL THINKING AND *GUNS, GERMS AND STEEL*

- Primary critical thinking skill: REASONING
- Secondary critical thinking skill: INTERPRETATION

In his 1997 work *Guns, Germs and Steel: The Fates of Human Societies*, Jared M. Diamond marshals evidence from five continents and across 13,000 years of human history in an attempt to answer the question of why that history unfolded so differently in various parts of the globe. His results offer new explanations for why the unequal divisions of power and wealth so familiar to us today came into existence—and have persisted.

Balancing materials drawn from a vast range of sources, addressing core problems that have fascinated historians, anthropologists, biologists and geographers alike—and blending his analysis to create a compelling narrative that became an international best-seller and reached a broad general market—required a mastery of the critical thinking skill of reasoning that few other scholars can rival. Diamond's reasoning skills allow him to persuade his readers of the value of his interdisciplinary approach and produce well-structured arguments that keep them turning pages even as he refocuses his analysis from one disparate example to another.

Diamond adds to that a spectacular ability to grasp the meaning of the available evidence produced by scholars in those widely different disciplines—making *Guns, Germs and Steel* equally valuable as an exercise in high-level interpretation.

《世界思想宝库钥匙丛书》简介

《世界思想宝库钥匙丛书》致力于为一系列在各领域产生重大影响的人文社科类经典著作提供独特的学术探讨。每一本读物都不仅仅是原经典著作的内容摘要，而是介绍并深入研究原经典著作的学术渊源、主要观点和历史影响。这一丛书的目的是提供一套学习资料，以促进读者掌握批判性思维，从而更全面、深刻地去理解重要思想。

每一本读物分为 3 个部分：学术渊源、学术思想和学术影响，每个部分下有 4 个小节。这些章节旨在从各个方面研究原经典著作及其反响。

由于独特的体例，每一本读物不但易于阅读，而且另有一项优点：所有读物的编排体例相同，读者在进行某个知识层面的调查或研究时可交叉参阅多本该丛书中的相关读物，从而开启跨领域研究的路径。

为了方便阅读，每本读物最后还列出了术语表和人名表（在书中则以星号 * 标记），此外还有参考文献。

《世界思想宝库钥匙丛书》与剑桥大学合作，理清了批判性思维的要点，即如何通过 6 种技能来进行有效思考。其中 3 种技能让我们能够理解问题，另 3 种技能让我们有能力解决问题。这 6 种技能合称为"批判性思维 PACIER 模式"，它们是：

分析：了解如何建立一个观点；

评估：研究一个观点的优点和缺点；

阐释：对意义所产生的问题加以理解；

创造性思维：提出新的见解，发现新的联系；

解决问题：提出切实有效的解决办法；

理性化思维：创建有说服力的观点。

THE MACAT LIBRARY

The Macat Library is a series of unique academic explorations of seminal works in the humanities and social sciences — books and papers that have had a significant and widely recognised impact on their disciplines. It has been created to serve as much more than just a summary of what lies between the covers of a great book. It illuminates and explores the influences on, ideas of, and impact of that book. Our goal is to offer a learning resource that encourages critical thinking and fosters a better, deeper understanding of important ideas.

Each publication is divided into three Sections: Influences, Ideas, and Impact. Each Section has four Modules. These explore every important facet of the work, and the responses to it.

This Section-Module structure makes a Macat Library book easy to use, but it has another important feature. Because each Macat book is written to the same format, it is possible (and encouraged!) to cross-reference multiple Macat books along the same lines of inquiry or research. This allows the reader to open up interesting interdisciplinary pathways.

To further aid your reading, lists of glossary terms and people mentioned are included at the end of this book (these are indicated by an asterisk [*] throughout) — as well as a list of works cited.

Macat has worked with the University of Cambridge to identify the elements of critical thinking and understand the ways in which six different skills combine to enable effective thinking.

Three allow us to fully understand a problem; three more give us the tools to solve it. Together, these six skills make up the PACIER model of critical thinking. They are:

ANALYSIS — understanding how an argument is built
EVALUATION — exploring the strengths and weaknesses of an argument
INTERPRETATION — understanding issues of meaning
CREATIVE THINKING — coming up with new ideas and fresh connections
PROBLEM-SOLVING — producing strong solutions
REASONING — creating strong arguments

"《世界思想宝库钥匙丛书》提供了独一无二的跨学科学习和研究工具。它介绍那些革新了各自学科研究的经典著作，还邀请全世界一流专家和教育机构进行严谨的分析，为每位读者打开世界顶级教育的大门。"

—— 安德烈亚斯·施莱歇尔，
经济合作与发展组织教育与技能司司长

"《世界思想宝库钥匙丛书》直面大学教育的巨大挑战……他们组建了一支精干而活跃的学者队伍，来推出在研究广度上颇具新意的教学材料。"

—— 布罗尔斯教授、勋爵，剑桥大学前校长

"《世界思想宝库钥匙丛书》的愿景令人赞叹。它通过分析和阐释那些曾深刻影响人类思想以及社会、经济发展的经典文本，提供了新的学习方法。它推动批判性思维，这对于任何社会和经济体来说都是至关重要的。这就是未来的学习方法。"

—— 查尔斯·克拉克阁下，英国前教育大臣

"对于那些影响了各自领域的著作，《世界思想宝库钥匙丛书》能让人们立即了解到围绕那些著作展开的评论性言论，这让该系列图书成为在这些领域从事研究的师生们不可或缺的资源。"

—— 威廉·特朗佐教授，加利福尼亚大学圣地亚哥分校

"Macat offers an amazing first-of-its-kind tool for interdisciplinary learning and research. Its focus on works that transformed their disciplines and its rigorous approach, drawing on the world's leading experts and educational institutions, opens up a world-class education to anyone."

—— Andreas Schleicher, Director for Education and Skills, Organisation for Economic Co-operation and Development

"Macat is taking on some of the major challenges in university education... They have drawn together a strong team of active academics who are producing teaching materials that are novel in the breadth of their approach."

—— Prof Lord Broers, former Vice-Chancellor of the University of Cambridge

"The Macat vision is exceptionally exciting. It focuses upon new modes of learning which analyse and explain seminal texts which have profoundly influenced world thinking and so social and economic development. It promotes the kind of critical thinking which is essential for any society and economy. This is the learning of the future."

—— Rt Hon Charles Clarke, former UK Secretary of State for Education

"The Macat analyses provide immediate access to the critical conversation surrounding the books that have shaped their respective discipline, which will make them an invaluable resource to all of those, students and teachers, working in the field."

—— Prof William Tronzo, University of California at San Diego

The Macat Library
世界思想宝库钥匙丛书

TITLE	中文书名	类别
An Analysis of Arjun Appadurai's *Modernity at Large: Cultural Dimensions of Globalization*	解析阿尔君·阿帕杜莱《消失的现代性：全球化的文化维度》	人类学
An Analysis of Claude Lévi-Strauss's *Structural Anthropology*	解析克劳德·列维-斯特劳斯《结构人类学》	人类学
An Analysis of Marcel Mauss's *The Gift*	解析马塞尔·莫斯《礼物》	人类学
An Analysis of Jared M. Diamond's *Guns, Germs, and Steel: The Fate of Human Societies*	解析贾雷德·M.戴蒙德《枪炮、病菌与钢铁：人类社会的命运》	人类学
An Analysis of Clifford Geertz's *The Interpretation of Cultures*	解析克利福德·格尔茨《文化的解释》	人类学
An Analysis of Philippe Ariès's *Centuries of Childhood: A Social History of Family Life*	解析菲力浦·阿利埃斯《儿童的世纪：旧制度下的儿童和家庭生活》	人类学
An Analysis of W. Chan Kim & Renée Mauborgne's *Blue Ocean Strategy*	解析金伟灿/勒妮·莫博涅《蓝海战略》	商业
An Analysis of John P. Kotter's *Leading Change*	解析约翰·P.科特《领导变革》	商业
An Analysis of Michael E. Porter's *Competitive Strategy: Techniques for Analyzing Industries and Competitors*	解析迈克尔·E.波特《竞争战略：分析产业和竞争对手的技术》	商业
An Analysis of Jean Lave & Etienne Wenger's *Situated Learning: Legitimate Peripheral Participation*	解析琼·莱夫/艾蒂纳·温格《情境学习：合法的边缘性参与》	商业
An Analysis of Douglas McGregor's *The Human Side of Enterprise*	解析道格拉斯·麦格雷戈《企业的人性面》	商业
An Analysis of Milton Friedman's *Capitalism and Freedom*	解析米尔顿·弗里德曼《资本主义与自由》	商业
An Analysis of Ludwig von Mises's *The Theory of Money and Credit*	解析路德维希·冯·米塞斯《货币和信用理论》	经济学
An Analysis of Adam Smith's *The Wealth of Nations*	解析亚当·斯密《国富论》	经济学
An Analysis of Thomas Piketty's *Capital in the Twenty-First Century*	解析托马斯·皮凯蒂《21世纪资本论》	经济学
An Analysis of Nassim Nicholas Taleb's *The Black Swan: The Impact of the Highly Improbable*	解析纳西姆·尼古拉斯·塔勒布《黑天鹅：如何应对不可预知的未来》	经济学
An Analysis of Ha-Joon Chang's *Kicking Away the Ladder*	解析张夏准《富国陷阱：发达国家为何踢开梯子》	经济学
An Analysis of Thomas Robert Malthus's *An Essay on the Principle of Population*	解析托马斯·罗伯特·马尔萨斯《人口论》	经济学

An Analysis of John Maynard Keynes's *The General Theory of Employment, Interest and Money*	解析约翰·梅纳德·凯恩斯《就业、利息和货币通论》	经济学
An Analysis of Milton Friedman's *The Role of Monetary Policy*	解析米尔顿·弗里德曼《货币政策的作用》	经济学
An Analysis of Burton G. Malkiel's *A Random Walk Down Wall Street*	解析伯顿·G. 马尔基尔《漫步华尔街》	经济学
An Analysis of Friedrich A. Hayek's *The Road to Serfdom*	解析弗里德里希·A. 哈耶克《通往奴役之路》	经济学
An Analysis of Charles P. Kindleberger's *Manias, Panics, and Crashes: A History of Financial Crises*	解析查尔斯·P. 金德尔伯格《疯狂、惊恐和崩溃：金融危机史》	经济学
An Analysis of Amartya Sen's *Development as Freedom*	解析阿马蒂亚·森《以自由看待发展》	经济学
An Analysis of Rachel Carson's *Silent Spring*	解析蕾切尔·卡森《寂静的春天》	地理学
An Analysis of Charles Darwin's *On the Origin of Species: by Means of Natural Selection, or The Preservation of Favoured Races in the Struggle for Life*	解析查尔斯·达尔文《物种起源》	地理学
An Analysis of World Commission on Environment and Development's *The Brundtland Report: Our Common Future*	解析世界环境与发展委员会《布伦特兰报告：我们共同的未来》	地理学
An Analysis of James E. Lovelock's *Gaia: A New Look at Life on Earth*	解析詹姆斯·E. 拉伍洛克《盖娅：地球生命的新视野》	地理学
An Analysis of Paul Kennedy's *The Rise and Fall of the Great Powers: Economic Change and Military Conflict from 1500–2000*	解析保罗·肯尼迪《大国的兴衰：1500—2000 年的经济变革与军事冲突》	历史
An Analysis of Janet L. Abu-Lughod's *Before European Hegemony: The World System A. D. 1250–1350*	解析珍妮特·L. 阿布–卢格霍德《欧洲霸权之前：1250—1350 年的世界体系》	历史
An Analysis of Alfred W. Crosby's *The Columbian Exchange: Biological and Cultural Consequences of 1492*	解析艾尔弗雷德·W. 克罗斯比《哥伦布大交换：1492 年以后的生物影响和文化冲击》	历史
An Analysis of Tony Judt's *Postwar: A History of Europe since 1945*	解析托尼·朱特《战后欧洲史》	历史
An Analysis of Richard J. Evans's *In Defence of History*	解析理查德·J. 艾文斯《捍卫历史》	历史
An Analysis of Eric Hobsbawm's *The Age of Revolution: Europe 1789–1848*	解析艾瑞克·霍布斯鲍姆《革命的年代：欧洲 1789—1848 年》	历史

An Analysis of Roland Barthes's *Mythologies*	解析罗兰·巴特《神话学》	文学与批判理论
An Analysis of Simone de Beauvoir's *The Second Sex*	解析西蒙娜·德·波伏娃《第二性》	文学与批判理论
An Analysis of Edward W. Said's *Orientalism*	解析爱德华·W.萨义德《东方主义》	文学与批判理论
An Analysis of Virginia Woolf's *A Room of One's Own*	解析弗吉尼亚·伍尔芙《一间自己的房间》	文学与批判理论
An Analysis of Judith Butler's *Gender Trouble*	解析朱迪斯·巴特勒《性别麻烦》	文学与批判理论
An Analysis of Ferdinand de Saussure's *Course in General Linguistics*	解析费尔迪南·德·索绪尔《普通语言学教程》	文学与批判理论
An Analysis of Susan Sontag's *On Photography*	解析苏珊·桑塔格《论摄影》	文学与批判理论
An Analysis of Walter Benjamin's *The Work of Art in the Age of Mechanical Reproduction*	解析瓦尔特·本雅明《机械复制时代的艺术作品》	文学与批判理论
An Analysis of W. E. B. Du Bois's *The Souls of Black Folk*	解析W.E.B.杜波依斯《黑人的灵魂》	文学与批判理论
An Analysis of Plato's *The Republic*	解析柏拉图《理想国》	哲学
An Analysis of Plato's *Symposium*	解析柏拉图《会饮篇》	哲学
An Analysis of Aristotle's *Metaphysics*	解析亚里士多德《形而上学》	哲学
An Analysis of Aristotle's *Nicomachean Ethics*	解析亚里士多德《尼各马可伦理学》	哲学
An Analysis of Immanuel Kant's *Critique of Pure Reason*	解析伊曼努尔·康德《纯粹理性批判》	哲学
An Analysis of Ludwig Wittgenstein's *Philosophical Investigations*	解析路德维希·维特根斯坦《哲学研究》	哲学
An Analysis of G. W. F. Hegel's *Phenomenology of Spirit*	解析G.W.F.黑格尔《精神现象学》	哲学
An Analysis of Baruch Spinoza's *Ethics*	解析巴鲁赫·斯宾诺莎《伦理学》	哲学
An Analysis of Hannah Arendt's *The Human Condition*	解析汉娜·阿伦特《人的境况》	哲学
An Analysis of G. E. M. Anscombe's *Modern Moral Philosophy*	解析G.E.M.安斯康姆《现代道德哲学》	哲学
An Analysis of David Hume's *An Enquiry Concerning Human Understanding*	解析大卫·休谟《人类理解研究》	哲学

An Analysis of Søren Kierkegaard's *Fear and Trembling*	解析索伦·克尔凯郭尔《恐惧与战栗》	哲学
An Analysis of René Descartes's *Meditations on First Philosophy*	解析勒内·笛卡尔《第一哲学沉思录》	哲学
An Analysis of Friedrich Nietzsche's *On the Genealogy of Morality*	解析弗里德里希·尼采《论道德的谱系》	哲学
An Analysis of Gilbert Ryle's *The Concept of Mind*	解析吉尔伯特·赖尔《心的概念》	哲学
An Analysis of Thomas Kuhn's *The Structure of Scientific Revolutions*	解析托马斯·库恩《科学革命的结构》	哲学
An Analysis of John Stuart Mill's *Utilitarianism*	解析约翰·斯图亚特·穆勒《功利主义》	哲学
An Analysis of Aristotle's *Politics*	解析亚里士多德《政治学》	政治学
An Analysis of Niccolò Machiavelli's *The Prince*	解析尼科洛·马基雅维利《君主论》	政治学
An Analysis of Karl Marx's *Capital*	解析卡尔·马克思《资本论》	政治学
An Analysis of Benedict Anderson's *Imagined Communities*	解析本尼迪克特·安德森《想象的共同体》	政治学
An Analysis of Samuel P. Huntington's *The Clash of Civilizations and the Remaking of World Order*	解析塞缪尔·P.亨廷顿《文明的冲突与世界秩序的重建》	政治学
An Analysis of Alexis de Tocqueville's *Democracy in America*	解析阿列克西·德·托克维尔《论美国的民主》	政治学
An Analysis of John A. Hobson's *Imperialism: A Study*	解析约翰·A.霍布森《帝国主义》	政治学
An Analysis of Thomas Paine's *Common Sense*	解析托马斯·潘恩《常识》	政治学
An Analysis of John Rawls's *A Theory of Justice*	解析约翰·罗尔斯《正义论》	政治学
An Analysis of Francis Fukuyama's *The End of History and the Last Man*	解析弗朗西斯·福山《历史的终结与最后的人》	政治学
An Analysis of John Locke's *Two Treatises of Government*	解析约翰·洛克《政府论》	政治学
An Analysis of Sun Tzu's *The Art of War*	解析孙武《孙子兵法》	政治学
An Analysis of Henry Kissinger's *World Order: Reflections on the Character of Nations and the Course of History*	解析亨利·基辛格《世界秩序》	政治学
An Analysis of Jean-Jacques Rousseau's *The Social Contract*	解析让-雅克·卢梭《社会契约论》	政治学

An Analysis of Odd Arne Westad's *The Global Cold War: Third World Interventions and the Making of Our Times*	解析文安立《全球冷战：美苏对第三世界的干涉与当代世界的形成》	政治学
An Analysis of Sigmund Freud's *The Interpretation of Dreams*	解析西格蒙德·弗洛伊德《梦的解析》	心理学
An Analysis of William James' *The Principles of Psychology*	解析威廉·詹姆斯《心理学原理》	心理学
An Analysis of Philip Zimbardo's *The Lucifer Effect*	解析菲利普·津巴多《路西法效应》	心理学
An Analysis of Leon Festinger's *A Theory of Cognitive Dissonance*	解析利昂·费斯汀格《认知失调论》	心理学
An Analysis of Richard H. Thaler & Cass R. Sunstein's *Nudge: Improving Decisions about Health, Wealth, and Happiness*	解析理查德·H. 泰勒 / 卡斯·R. 桑斯坦《助推：如何做出有关健康、财富和幸福的更优决策》	心理学
An Analysis of Gordon Allport's *The Nature of Prejudice*	解析高尔登·奥尔波特《偏见的本质》	心理学
An Analysis of Steven Pinker's *The Better Angels of Our Nature: Why Violence Has Declined*	解析斯蒂芬·平克《人性中的善良天使：暴力为什么会减少》	心理学
An Analysis of Stanley Milgram's *Obedience to Authority*	解析斯坦利·米尔格拉姆《对权威的服从》	心理学
An Analysis of Betty Friedan's *The Feminine Mystique*	解析贝蒂·弗里丹《女性的奥秘》	心理学
An Analysis of David Riesman's *The Lonely Crowd: A Study of the Changing American Character*	解析大卫·理斯曼《孤独的人群：美国人社会性格演变之研究》	社会学
An Analysis of Franz Boas's *Race, Language and Culture*	解析弗朗兹·博厄斯《种族、语言与文化》	社会学
An Analysis of Pierre Bourdieu's *Outline of a Theory of Practice*	解析皮埃尔·布尔迪厄《实践理论大纲》	社会学
An Analysis of Max Weber's *The Protestant Ethic and the Spirit of Capitalism*	解析马克斯·韦伯《新教伦理与资本主义精神》	社会学
An Analysis of Jane Jacobs's *The Death and Life of Great American Cities*	解析简·雅各布斯《美国大城市的死与生》	社会学
An Analysis of C. Wright Mills's *The Sociological Imagination*	解析 C. 赖特·米尔斯《社会学的想象力》	社会学
An Analysis of Robert E. Lucas Jr.'s *Why Doesn't Capital Flow from Rich to Poor Countries?*	解析小罗伯特·E. 卢卡斯《为何资本不从富国流向穷国？》	社会学

An Analysis of Émile Durkheim's *On Suicide*	解析埃米尔·迪尔凯姆《自杀论》	社会学
An Analysis of Eric Hoffer's *The True Believer: Thoughts on the Nature of Mass Movements*	解析埃里克·霍弗《狂热分子：群众运动圣经》	社会学
An Analysis of Jared M. Diamond's *Collapse: How Societies Choose to Fail or Survive*	解析贾雷德·M. 戴蒙德《大崩溃：社会如何选择兴亡》	社会学
An Analysis of Michel Foucault's *The History of Sexuality Vol. 1: The Will to Knowledge*	解析米歇尔·福柯《性史（第一卷）：求知意志》	社会学
An Analysis of Michel Foucault's *Discipline and Punish*	解析米歇尔·福柯《规训与惩罚》	社会学
An Analysis of Richard Dawkins's *The Selfish Gene*	解析理查德·道金斯《自私的基因》	社会学
An Analysis of Antonio Gramsci's *Prison Notebooks*	解析安东尼奥·葛兰西《狱中札记》	社会学
An Analysis of Augustine's *Confessions*	解析奥古斯丁《忏悔录》	神学
An Analysis of C. S. Lewis's *The Abolition of Man*	解析 C. S. 路易斯《人之废》	神学

图书在版编目（CIP）数据

解析贾雷德·M.戴蒙德《枪炮、病菌与钢铁：人类社会的命运》：
汉、英 / 赖利·恩 (Riley Quinn) 著；赵婧译. -- 上海：上海外语教育
出版社, 2020 (2022重印)
（世界思想宝库钥匙丛书）
ISBN 978-7-5446-6388-5

Ⅰ.①解… Ⅱ.①莱… ②赵… Ⅲ.①社会发展史－研究－世界－
汉、英 Ⅳ.①K02

中国版本图书馆CIP数据核字（2020）第057288号

This Chinese-English bilingual edition of *An Analysis of Jared M. Diamond's* Guns, Germs, and Steel The Fate of Human Societies is published by arrangement with Macat International Limited.

Licensed for sale throughout the world.

本书汉英双语版由Macat国际有限公司授权上海外语教育出版社有限公司出版。
供在全世界范围内发行、销售。

图字：09 - 2018 - 549

出版发行：**上海外语教育出版社**
　　　　　　　（上海外国语大学内）　邮编：200083
电　　话：021-65425300（总机）
电子邮箱：bookinfo@sflep.com.cn
网　　址：http://www.sflep.com
责任编辑：蒋怡颖

印　　刷：上海叶大印务发展有限公司
开　　本：890×1240　1/32　印张 5.625　字数 116千字
版　　次：2020 年 9 月第 1 版　　2022 年 12 月第 2 次印刷

书　　号：ISBN 978-7-5446-6388-5
定　　价：30.00 元
　　本版图书如有印装质量问题，可向本社调换
　　质量服务热线：4008-213-263　电子邮箱：editorial@sflep.com